Western
CIVILIZATION II

CLEP* Study Guide

© 2013 Breely Crush Publishing, LLC

*CLEP is a registered trademark of the College Entrance Examination Board which does not endorse this book.

971092712143

Published by Breely Crush Publishing, LLC
10808 River Front Parkway
South Jordan, UT 84095
www.breelycrushpublishing.com

ISBN-10: 1-61433-032-8
ISBN-13: 978-1-61433-032-5

Printed and bound in the United States of America.

*CLEP is a registered trademark of the College Entrance Examination Board which does not endorse this book.

Table of Contents

Western Civilization Since 1648

Since 1648, Western civilization has led the world in many respects. Often that leadership came in the form of discovery, whether that was new lands, new scientific advancements, or new ideas. Sometimes that leadership came from political ideologies that clashed, thereby leading to war. The history of the modern West, therefore, is both captivating and tragic.

Absolutionism and Constitutionalism, 1648-1715

The growth of nation-states in Western Europe began as feudalism declined. England and France had developed into highly centralized nation-states by 1500. Spain, only recently unified politically, rapidly and aggressively consolidated royal power, using the influence of the Catholic Church. Their governments were under the leadership of strong rulers, who often reigned as absolute monarchs, that is, the king or queen had complete or absolute rule over the nation and its subjects. Such monarchs are also called autocrats, and their governments are referred to as autocracies.

In Central and Eastern Europe, ethnic and cultural diversity impeded the development of nation-states based on commonalities of language and tradition. The shifting boundaries of the Holy Roman Empire and the widespread holdings of the Habsburg dynasty created more loosely knit political units resistant to centralization. In addition, the power of the landowning nobility in these areas had been reasserted at the expense of both monarchs and the urban middle class. Unlike the west where the peasantry had maintained the social and economic gains of the late Middle Ages, eastern peasants succumbed to the concerted efforts of landowners to reestablish serfdom.

The Dutch Republic

The first European society to throw off the yoke of a powerful central state, and then to adopt a constitutional republic, was the Netherlands. After decades of resistance against Spanish domination of the "northern provinces," the United Provinces, or the Dutch Republic, gained recognition of their status from the Spanish crown in 1609. Even so, it was not until the Peace of Westphalia (1648), ending the Thirty Years War, that Dutch independence was confirmed. Dutch political and economic success was grounded in hardheaded practicality and a fierce sense of independence. The government of the United Provinces was unique in Europe, a republic dominated by prosperous middle class merchants who valued thrift, diligence, and simplicity. It was unique, too, because toleration became a cornerstone of Dutch political and economic practice. In a practical sense, toleration attracted investors of all faiths and backgrounds, and the Netherlands profited greatly from this. They also benefited greatly from dominating trade from a neutral status when other European powers were expending finances and resources for warfare on the continent and in overseas colonies. During the remainder of the seventeenth century, the Dutch example would serve as a model for scores of constitution-minded people of northern and western Europeans.

France

While the Dutch were moving away from central power, the French experienced a massive expansion of the state's authority. After the Hundred Years War, royal power in France became more centralized. In addition to the rulers of the 1500s who steadily assumed more authority for the crown, as adviser to Louis XIII, Cardinal Richelieu (1624-1642), Richelieu laid the foundations for a strong French monarchy by weakening the nobles and increasing taxes. Richelieu made the monarchy absolute within France, and his foreign policy made France the strongest power in Europe.

By the mid-1600s King Louis XIV (1643–1715), who was known as the Sun King, ruled as an absolute monarch. Louis XIV believed in the divine right theory of government, which held that a monarch's power came from God and that the monarch was accountable not to the people he ruled but only to God. Louis also used his wealth for his own benefit rather than for the people. The great palace at Versailles, near Paris, was built at his direction. The construction of the palace seemed to support his statement: "L'étât, c'est moi" (I am the state). Not surprisingly, Louis XIV never summoned the Estates-General (the French congress) to meet.

Louis' absolutism also involved waging wars. He led France into many wars, hoping to gain territory. Few of these were successful, and their major result was to increase the dissatisfaction of the French people because of many deaths and high taxes. His control over the French economy was aided by the actions of his finance minister, Jean Colbert.

Louis did promote artistic and musical works to glorify his rule, and he made France the cultural center of Europe. These activities also increased the spirit of French nationalism. Finally, he revoked the Edict of Nantes, which was a blow to religious freedom and forced many Huguenots to leave France. The absolutism in England and France eventually sparked strong political reactions and resulted in important democratic developments.

England

Following Queen Elizabeth I were the rulers of the Stuart Dynasty (1603–1649), James I and Charles I. They ruled as absolute monarchs, believing they should have no limits set on their power. The Stuart rulers did not respect previous democratic traditions and preferred to rule by divine right. They came into conflict with Parliament because they disregarded it in raising money, imprisoned people unfairly, and persecuted Puritans. However, the underlying conflict was the question of where power would be centered—in the monarchy or in the Parliament.

In 1640, when Scotland invaded England, Charles was forced to call Parliament into session. Led by Puritans, this Parliament, which sat from 1640 to 1660, is known as the Long Parliament, and it changed English history by limiting the absolute powers of the monarchy. In 1641 Parliament denied Charles's request for money to raise an army to fight the Irish rebellion. In response, Charles led troops into the House of Commons to arrest some of its Puritan members. The attempt by Charles to arrest members of Parliament sparked the beginning of the English Civil War (1642-45), as Parliament soon raised an army to fight the king. The Parliamentary forces emerged victorious under the leadership of Oliver Cromwell, a Puritan.

The subsequent Puritan Revolution (1642–1660) included the rule by Oliver Cromwell, which began in 1649. Under Cromwell's leadership, the Parliament voted to abolish the monarchy, and Charles I was tried and beheaded in 1649. England was now a republic or, as it called itself, a commonwealth. However, in 1653, supported by his army, Cromwell took the title of Lord Protector and ruled as a military dictator. His dictatorial policies, which included religious intolerance, strict moral codes, and violence against the Irish, caused resentment. Soon after his death, Parliament invited Charles II, the son of Charles I who was in exile, to take the throne.

Aware of English democratic traditions and the fate of his father, Charles II was careful not to anger Parliament. He acknowledged the rights of the people established by the Magna Carta and the Petition of Right. In 1679, he agreed to the Habeas Corpus Act. On his death in 1685, his brother James II became king. James angered Parliament because of his pro-Catholic actions and his claim to divine right rule. Parliament invited James's older daughter, Mary, and her husband, William of Orange, a Dutch prince who was Protestant, to take the throne.

William and Mary accepted Parliament's offer and arrived in England with an army. They were proclaimed king and queen, as James II fled to France. As a result of this bloodless revolution, which is known as the Glorious Revolution, Parliament gained in power and prestige. To protect its newly won supremacy over the monarchy, Parliament passed a Bill of Rights that was signed by William and Mary in 1689. Thus, by the end of the 17th century, England had become a limited, or constitutional, monarchy, the first in Europe. All the major decisions were made by Parliament, and the ruler's actions were limited by Parliament.

Formation of Austria and Prussia

Even though absolutism developed later in Eastern Europe, it proved more enduring, resisting democratic and Enlightenment ideas more rigorously right down to the First World War. Weakened by the religious strife in the north during the early 17th century, Austrian rulers of the Holy Roman Empire focused on their lands to the east and south. Ferdinand II (1619–1637) put down a revolt in Bohemia by Czech nobles, redistributed their land, and stamped out Protestantism in the area. Ferdinand III centralized government administration in Austria itself and created a standing army for both defense and domestic control. When the Ottoman siege of Vienna failed in 1683, the Habsburgs, with Russian and other allies, pushed the Turks back and by 1699 controlled Hungary and a large part of Romania.

Complete autocratic centralization was never possible, however, in part because of the vigorous independence of the Hungarian nobility and the lack of a unifying language and culture. Charles VI attempted to guarantee the unity of the three Habsburg realms (Bohemia, Austria, and Hungary) proclaiming in the Pragmatic Sanction (1713) that they should never be divided. The Estates of the three areas, particularly Hungary, continued to strive for influence and resist the power of the crown.

How did a small, landlocked, and relatively unproductive north German kingdom become the core of a militant and powerful empire? The tiny state of Brandenburg, overrun by Swedish and Habsburg armies during the Thirty Years War, and Prussia, tributary state to the King of Poland, were united in 1618 by the Hohenzollern rulers. Formerly a bit player on the stage of the Holy Roman Empire, this dynasty's fortunes changed with the accession to the throne in 1640 of Frederick William, who came to be known as the Great Elector. Taking advantage of an aristocracy weakened by religious wars, and supported by a population tired of the depredations of the marauding armies of Sweden and Poland, he established a standing army and exacted taxes to pay for it. By his death in 1688, Frederick William had consolidated his widely separated lands into a viable, but still small and weak German-speaking kingdom.

It was left to his near-namesake, King Frederick William I (1713–1740) to imbue this new nation-state with an element of his own concept of political power as a function of military might. His strong centralized bureaucracy, coupled with the size and strength of his army precluded significant opposition. He overcame opposition from the great landowning aristocracy of Prussia, the Junkers, by co-opting them into the officer corps, giving them military as well as economic power over other groups in the society. By 1740, Prussia, which ranked twelfth in population, had Europe's fourth largest army—only those of France, Austria, and Russia were larger.

Thus, the "Sparta of the North," as some historians have called it, became a militaristic society where obedience became the primary virtue of the ordinary citizen as well as of the officer or soldier. The precision, skill, and discipline of the Prussian military became the envy of others, and for the next two centuries Prussian arms nearly always prevailed when put to the test of battle.

The "Westernization" of Russia

Under Peter I, usually referred to as "the Great," Russia underwent important changes. Following a policy of Westernization in order to modernize his nation, Peter forced the nobility and upper classes to imitate their counterparts in Western Europe socially and culturally. A Western European-style bourgeoisie (urban middle class) was also created. An enormous civil service and government bureaucracy that drew from both the upper and middle classes was established. Peter encouraged the development of new industries and the importation of Westerners to train Russians. A new capital city, St. Petersburg, was built on the Baltic. Known as the "Window to the West," St. Petersburg was modeled after Western European cities. The Patriarchate was abolished and replaced with the Synod (Council) of Bishops under the control of a Procurator (one of the tsar's ministers).

The education system, once administered by the Church, was also taken over by the state. The army was modernized, the latest weapons technology imported, and a navy was created. Under Peter, Russia expanded westward to the Baltic and southeast to the Black Sea. For the first time in history, the nation of Russia was no longer landlocked, although both water routes were limited. Even though most of the population were peasants and remained unaffected by the Petrine Reforms, Russia was transformed into a modern world power.

Competition for Empire and Economic Expansion

During the eighteenth century the major European powers—Spain, the Netherlands, France, and England—all worked to expand their territorial holdings in the Americas, Africa, and Asia. That geopolitical contest was deemed crucial because of the economic benefits of producing raw goods from far-flung colonies. As a result, each nation attempted to gain new lands of the others, which in turn produced a series of large-scale wars that not only affected the continent of Europe but also colonies in the Americas and Asia.

Global Economy of the 18th Century

Between the late sixteenth and early nineteenth centuries, the Dutch, French, and English sought to establish colonies in the Americas. They took possession of territory primarily in the Caribbean region and along the northeastern coast of South America. By the eighteenth century, an intricate system of trade among the continents of North America, South America, Africa, and Europe was in place. Generally, Europeans extracted—often through slave labor—raw goods from their colonies in the Americas, and in turn sold finished goods to their colonists across the Atlantic. This system of increasing the size of the economy of the "mother country" by extracting raw goods from colonies was called mercantilism. The establishment of a plantation economy, based on slave labor and restrictive mercantilist trade policies, was promoted by all of the major European powers.

Besides the settlements along the eastern coast of North America, the British were also able to establish themselves throughout the Caribbean. Jamaica, Barbados, and Trinidad-Tobago were their principal possessions in what became the British West Indies in the late 1600s. As elsewhere in the Caribbean, large numbers of African slaves were brought in to provide labor for the sugar-cane plantations in the British West Indies. The first English settlements of South America, in present-day Guyana, began in the 1600s. The English, French, and Dutch colonies in the Caribbean basin all developed a highly profitable sugar-cane-plantation economy, utilizing imported African slave labor. The colonies were controlled by trading policies that favored the "mother" country. The European colonial powers exploited the resources of the Caribbean Islands to further their own economic development. As a result, European nation-states funded their own hyper-expansionist tendencies of the eighteenth century with profits gleaned from their overseas ventures.

Europe after Utrecht, 1713-1740

The importance of North American possessions—and, especially, the wealth produced from their soils—became obvious when European nations began a long series of wars that in part were caused by territorial questions across the Atlantic. To be sure, especially for the British, these wars were driven by the theory of mercantilism. As both France and Britain jockeyed for dominance in North America, those wars were fought by countries who took either the French or British side.

The first conflict was the War of the Spanish Succession, which resulted in major gains for Great Britain in the Peace of Utrecht. France ceded Newfoundland, Nova Scotia, and the Hudson Bay territory to Britain. Spain was compelled to give Britain control of the lucrative West African slave trade—the so-called asiento—and to let Britain send one ship of merchandise into the Spanish colonies annually.

Though the post-Utrecht peace was maintained for thirty years, by mid-century the European powers were determined to achieve territorial and economic gains at the expense of the others. The decisive round in the French-British competition was the Seven Years' War (1756-1763), which caused France to lose all of its North American possessions. By 1763, therefore, Britain had realized its goal of monopolizing a vast trade and colonial empire for its benefit.

 # Demographic Change in the 18th Century

This interconnected expansion of trade and empire marked a major step toward the Industrial Revolution, although people could not know it at the time. In turn, some key demographic processes were set afoot that would dramatically alter Western societies. Because Britain became the world's first industrialized nation, and because population growth attended industrialization in most countries, Britain's population grew steadily during the late eighteenth and nineteenth centuries. Fed by the agricultural revolution of the eighteenth century, the British—and then workers in other Western societies—came to build an increasingly improved quality of life.

 # The Scientific View of the World

The two most important intellectual developments of this era were the Scientific Revolution and the Enlightenment. Scientists' and theorists' concern with natural rights and the use of reason, logic, and experience was seen in the field of science as well as in politics and economics. During the 16th and 17th centuries, the way the people of Europe viewed themselves and the universe underwent a dramatic transformation in what was called the Scientific Revolution. The discoveries of a succession of astronomers, physicists, and mathematicians undermined many ideas that had been accepted for centuries. A new system of ideas and theories was created, based on the direct observation of nature and a belief in the power of reason.

Major Figures of the Scientific Revolution

The scientific method, based on carefully planned experiments, observation of results, and the formulation of general laws, was the basis of the Scientific Revolution. Scientists such as Isaac Newton (1642–1727) of England used the scientific method to investigate nature. Newton, the leading figure in the Scientific Revolution, put forth important theories about gravity and the movement of planets. His famous book was the Principia Mathematica.

Other figures were crucial to the development of this scientific thought. Francis Bacon, Nicholas Copernicus, Rene Descartes, and Galileo Galilei—as well as a host of less famous scientists—updated the world's understanding of mathematics, astronomy, biology, chemistry, and physics. As a result, collectively, the major figures of the Scientific Revolution would have an immense social and political impact on future generations.

 # New Knowledge of Man and Society

Thus, the Scientific Revolution gave the western world the impression that the human mind was progressing toward some ultimate end. Thanks to the culminating work of Newton, the western intellectual tradition now included a firm believe in the idea of human progress, that is, that man's history could be identified as the progressive unfolding of man's capacity for perfectibility. From this point on, man the believer was now joined by man the knower. It was man's destiny to both know the world, and create that world. But, the Scientific Revolution also showed man to be merely a small part of a larger divine plan. Man no longer found himself at the center of the universe—he was now simply a small part of a much greater whole.

 # Political Theory

As science revealed more of the extent and workings of the physical universe, the God of the Judeo-Christian tradition became less compatible with the emergent picture of the cosmos and the laws of nature. Inductive science slowed overcame deductive logic. The kingdom of man challenged the kingdom of God. Nature came to be regarded as a complicated and impressive affair. Simple biblical explanations of the cosmos and Nature were no longer satisfied the best minds of Europe. God was portrayed as a law-giving and law-abiding being but natural causes were sought to explain the workings of the natural world.

Man was still believed to possess an immortal soul. But the natural philosophers were no longer willing to let man pass merely as the image of God. Among advanced thinkers, morality was gradually divorced from the supernatural conception of sin and related to behavior on this earth and its effects upon the individual and society. Some of the more secular trends in humanism dared to defend happiness in the here and now.

Among political theorists who wrote during the Scientific Revolution, a new optimism regarding the future of man came into being and helped to produce the notion that man was indeed a progressive being and that perfectibility was perhaps possible in Western societies. The exploration of lands outside Europe brought new information, revealed new and diverse ways of life, stimulated curiosity and developed the comparative approach towards customs and institutions. A new world view was the result.
Consequently, some of the West's most important political theories grew out of the scientific age. Michel de Montaigne, Thomas Hobbes, and John Locke all dominated the political thinking of the sixteenth and seventeenth centuries, with Locke serving as a bridge between the Scientific Revolution and subsequent Enlightenment. Locke argued that philosophy should pretend to deal only with problems and conceptions that the human mind is capable of encompassing.

Admitting definite limitations to the human mind, he excluded from consideration many issues which earlier philosophers and theologians had attempted to meddle with. Locke directed his heaviest fire against the doctrine that ideas are inherent at birth in the human mind and that they are not to be tampered with except on pain of upsetting the natural constitution of society. In attempting to combat this notion, he used the notion of the tabula rasa (blank slate) to signify the condition of the mind at birth. This idea would help to build the foundation of the Enlightenment.

 # *Period of Enlightenment*

The Enlightenment, also called the Age of Reason, was an intellectual movement in the 17th and 18th centuries. The scientific and intellectual developments of the 17th century—the discoveries of Isaac Newton, the rationalism of Réné Descartes, the skepticism of Pierre Bayle, the pantheism of Benedict de Spinoza, and the empiricism of Francis Bacon and John Locke—fostered the belief in natural law and universal order and the confidence in human reason that spread to influence all of 18th-century society. Currents of thought in the Enlightenment were varied, but certain ideas may be characterized as pervading and dominant. A rational and scientific approach to religious, social, political, and economic issues promoted a secular view of the world and a general sense of progress and perfectibility.

Enlightenment Thought

The Enlightenment was sparked by the progress of the Scientific Revolution. Educated Europeans had learned that natural laws governed the physical universe. They reasoned that similar laws must govern human society as well. If people were able to discover these laws, they might be used to construct a better government and more just societies. The thinkers, philosophers, and writers who examined the political and social problems of the time were known as philosophes. They believed that everything, even government and religion, should be open to reason and criticism. They were convinced that through the use of reason, logic, and experience, people could improve their society—its laws, economy, and so on. The philosophes claimed that humans had certain natural rights. Traditional royal and Church authority, particularly in France, were in conflict with these rights and had to undergo change.

Some of the most important writers of the Enlightenment were French—a fact not coincidental to the onset of the French Revolution. For example, Montesquieu (1689-1755), in his Spirit of the Laws, argued that there should be a separation of powers in government as well as a system of checks and balances. These features would prevent tyranny and absolutism. Likewise, Voltaire (1694-1778), in his Letters Concerning the English, supported the concepts of England's limited monarchy and its ideas on freedom of speech and religion. The Social Contract, written by Rousseau (1712-1778), argued that inequality among people can be ended by citizens coming together and agreeing to a general will. The general will is what the majority desires and should be carried out by the government. Finally, Diderot (1713-1784), in his far-reaching Encyclopedia, contended that absolutism and the injustices of the Old Regime were wrong. Together, these writers and their ideas would underlay the subsequent age of revolution.

There were also other important Enlightenment writers. Adam Smith of England (The Wealth of Nations) said that people should be free to conduct business without government interference. This was the laissez-faire philosophy of economics. The American Thomas Paine (Common Sense) claimed that it was right and natural for the American colonists to revolt against England, a tyrannical government that was thousands of miles across the Atlantic Ocean. John Locke was also a major Enlightenment writer.

Enlightened Despotism

Encouraged and instructed by the philosophes, many absolutist rulers of the later eighteenth century tried to govern in an "enlightened" manner. Yet the actual programs and accomplishments of these rulers varied greatly. Both in small states and in large states, individual rulers tried to apply the teachings of the philosophes to their public policy agendas. Most prominent in doing so were the leaders of Prussia, Russia, and Austria.

Frederick the Great of Prussia is regarded as being the most committed of the enlightened despots. In addition to his vigorous military campaigns that expanded Prussian control over eastern Europe, Frederick instituted many social and cultural advances at home that improved the lives of average Prussians. Frederick sponsored concerts and intellectual symposia that indicated the Prussian state's commitment to the Enlightenment. Politically, however, Frederick's reforms stopped short of reordering Prussian society, most notably the system of serfdom that had existed for centuries.

Likewise, Catherine the Great of Russia was an enlightened despot whose reforms were forward-thinking but still limited. Adored by the philosophes, Catherine worked tirelessly to continue the process of westernization; she purchases scores of prominent works of art, and even sent money to sponsor notable figures of the Enlightenment. After reforming Russia's legal code, Catherine followed Frederick's example of territorial expansion.

On a smaller level, in Austria, Joseph II (1780-1790) continued the limited enlightened rule of his mother, Maria Theresa (1740-1780). Though the kind of large-scale social reordering that philosophes espoused did not result, Joseph did succeed in streamlining the central government's bureaucracy.

Partition of Poland

One irony of the similar aims of Frederick the Great of Prussia and Catherine the Great of Russia was that their programs of territorial expansion met in Poland. Catherine's greatest coup was the partitioning of Poland, whose fate in the late eighteenth century demonstrated the dangers of failing to build a strong absolutist state. All important decisions continued to require the unanimous agreement of all nobles elected to the Polish Diet, which meant that nothing could ever be done to strengthen the state. When Frederick the Great proposed that Prussia, Austria, and Russia each take a gigantic slice of Polish territory, Catherine jumped at the chance. The first partition of Poland took place in 1772. Two more partitions, in 1793 and 1795, gave all three powers more Polish territory, and the ancient republic of Poland simply vanished from the map.

Revolution and Napoleonic Europe

The last years of the eighteenth century were a time of great upheaval in the West. A series of revolutions and revolutionary wars challenged the old order of monarchs and aristocrats. The ideas of freedom and equality flourished and spread. The revolutionary era began in North America in 1775, and then spread to France in 1789. France eventually established a constitutional monarchy, and then a radical republic, only to become an empire under Napoleon by the end of the century. The armies of France also joined forces with patriots and radicals abroad in an effort to establish throughout much of Europe new governments based on new principles.

The Revolution in France

In 1789 King Louis XVI called the Estates-General into session because he needed money to solve France's financial problems. This was the first time this body had been summoned since 1614 (175 years before). When the Estates-General met, the Third Estate refused to accept the traditional method of voting—each estate met separately and had one vote—because it would be outvoted by the other two estates. It demanded that all three estates meet together and that each deputy have a vote. When the king refused, the Third Estate, on June 17, 1789, declared itself to be the National Assembly and in the Tennis Court Oath pledged to write a constitution for the nation. This declaration was the beginning of the French Revolution.

On July 14, 1789, the revolution spread as a mob stormed and destroyed the Bastille—a prison that was a symbol of the Old Regime. The next day the king recognized the National Assembly. The National Assembly, which was made up of moderates, took power and began to carry out reforms. They passed the Declaration of the Rights of Man on August 27, 1789. This document was similar to the American Declaration of Independence and the English Bill of Rights. It stated the following democratic ideals: (1) class structure and privileges connected with the three estates were ended, abolishing the remains of feudalism; (2) all people were equal before the law and had certain basic freedoms, including freedom of religion, speech, and the press; and (3) the spirit of "Liberty, Equality, and Fraternity" was to guide the nation.

In 1790 the National Assembly abolished the special taxes and privileges of the Catholic Church in the Civil Constitution of the Clergy. It also granted freedom of worship, confiscated all Church land, and placed the Church under the government's control. The French Constitution was written in 1791, and it created a limited, or constitutional, monarchy and established separate executive, legislative, and judicial branches of government. However, King Louis's unsuccessful attempt to flee the country and war with Austria and Prussia enabled radicals, such as Robespierre, Danton, and Marat, to take over the Revolution. In 1792 delegates were elected by universal manhood suffrage to the National Convention, which took the place of the National Assembly and contained more radical members, such as the Jacobins. The first act of the National Convention was to declare France a republic. Louis XVI was brought to trial and executed in 1792.

The National Convention was soon taken over by extremist groups, who formed the Committee of Public Safety, which put the executive, legislative, and judicial powers of government in the hands of a small group of revolutionaries. The committee was given power to conduct the war with France's enemies and to enforce the ideals of the Revolution by all means possible. The leading figures were Danton and Robespierre, who began a Reign of Terror (1793–1794) in which they executed at the guillotine all enemies of the revolution, who were to them the nobles or anybody who spoke out against them. Eventually, more moderate groups, anti-Jacobins, took over the National Convention. Danton and Robespierre were themselves sentenced to die by the guillotine in 1795.

The Convention wrote a new constitution in 1795 that made France a republic. It established a five-member Directory government that ruled France until 1799, when it was replaced by the military dictatorship of Napoleon Bonaparte. This return of government to moderate control is called the Thermidorian Reaction.

The Revolution and Europe

The French Revolution had many important and long-lasting results. It brought about a basic change in the relationship between the government and the governed. Along with the revolutions in England and the United States, the French Revolution advanced democracy by recognizing the value and worth of the individual. Political power passed from an absolutist monarch who ruled by Divine Right and the nobles to the masses of people. A greater sense of nationalism and patriotism developed. Also, the remaining feudal features of French society were removed. The growing power of the bourgeoisie helped France to become a strong capitalist nation.

Bourgeoisie is a term evolved from French which has come to describe the working or capitalist class. In France before the French Revolution the bourgeoisie were the rising merchant class who found themselves suppressed by the aristocracy, whose wealth was a product of birth rather than merit. At the time the population of France was structured into three social classes: the First Estate was the clergy, the Second Estate was the aristocracy, or ruling class, and the Third Estate comprised everyone else – the wealthier end of which would have been the bourgeoisie. Although the Third Estate described

95% of the population, they had few rights. The bourgeoisie were the main leaders of the French Revolution who were disgusted by the attitudes of the aristocracy and their treatment of the Third Estate.

The French Empire

Napoleon Bonaparte was an ambitious, brilliant military officer who won many victories in wars against France's enemies. In 1799 in a coup d'etat (a sudden takeover of a government), he came to power in France in a new government called the Consulate. The Directory had lost support because of worsening economic problems and its inability to defeat Russia and Austria in the war. The Consulate was headed by three consuls, with Napoleon as First Consul. The new government, France's fourth in ten years, was called a republic, but it was a military dictatorship under the control of Napoleon. He took the title of Emperor Napoleon I in 1804.

By 1806 Napoleon had managed to conquer most of mainland Europe, and so he set his sights on Britain. Because his navy had recently been destroyed it was not feasible for him to launch an actual attack, and instead he turned to an economic solution termed the Continental System. The idea of this system was to end all trade with Britain, forcing them into a depression and giving him the upper hand. Napoleon ordered that all other countries join him in his endeavor (which they were for the most part willing to do). The system was fairly effective in the sense that it did cause inflation and bankruptcies in Britain. However, it also had negative impacts on French businesses. Within a few years, Napoleon was forced to allow trade with Britain in an effort to raise gold which he desperately needed.

The French people accepted his ruthless methods because they believed he would bring peace and stability to the nation. At first, Napoleon was brilliantly successful in his war against France's European enemies. Under Napoleon's leadership, French forces won victories and took large amounts of land in Europe. By 1808 Napoleon dominated Europe, and he reorganized many parts of Europe, making members of his family rulers in Italy, Spain, and other places.

The Napoleonic Empire soon became too large to control, however, and in time Napoleon suffered severe military setbacks. His attempt to conquer Russia in 1812 failed due to the harsh winter conditions and the scorched-earth fighting tactics of the Russians. At the Battle of Waterloo in 1815, fought near Brussels in Belgium, Napoleon's forces were defeated by the combined forces of European nations led by the Duke of Wellington of Britain.

Napoleon made many significant contributions to governing France. Both within France and in the areas he conquered, Napoleon sought to carry out the ideals of the French Revolution as he interpreted them. Indeed, he called himself a son of the Revolution and carried out a number of reforms. First, the Code Napoleon brought all the laws, regulations, and reforms of the revolution into a single system of law. Based on the belief that all people are equal before the law, the Napoleonic Code became the fundamental law of France and the parts of Europe governed by France.

Next, the Concordat of 1801 provided for a peaceful relationship between the French government and the Catholic Church. This converged with an efficient, centralized government that was created in France, with specific power over the education and banking systems. Government officials were selected based on merit through an examination system, and a public school system was established.
Napoleon's reforms also impacted people outside of France, as many European monarchs lost their thrones to Napoleon's armies. Peoples in these areas, such as Spain and Italy, learned of the ideals of the French Revolution. At first, some of these people welcomed Napoleon because they believed he had liberated them from foreign and unjust rule.

Eventually, they turned against Napoleon's dictatorial rule and fought against him, ultimately leading to his defeat in 1815. In any case, as a result of Napoleon's conquests, the ideas of the French Revolution were spread throughout Europe. The ideals of social justice, liberty, and democracy became rallying cries for reformers. Combined with the rise of the spirit of nationalism, which was stirred by the struggle against Napoleon's armies, the dreams of liberty and equality made many national groups determined to gain self-government in the years after 1815.

Congress of Vienna

After Napoleon's defeat, five major European powers—England, Russia, Prussia, France, and Austria—met at the Congress of Vienna in 1814 and 1815 to draw up peace plans and settle a number of important territorial questions by redrawing the map of Europe. Under the leadership of Austria's Count Metternich, the Congress of Vienna sought to restore political life in Europe, including former rulers and boundaries, to what it had been prior to Napoleon and to maintain peace and stability. Such a policy of restoring past ways and turning the clock back is called reactionary. Metternich wanted to wipe out the ideas spread by the Napoleonic era and return to the old days of absolutism and special privilege. The decisions reached at the Congress of Vienna were based on three principles—legitimacy, the balance of power, and compensation.

Legitimacy meant restoring the ruling families that reigned before the French Revolution to their thrones. Balance of power meant that no one nation should be strong enough to threaten the security of the others. To do this, shifts of territory were necessary. This involved compensation, or providing one state with territory to pay for territory taken away from that state.

The principle results of the conference were that France was stripped of the lands that it had acquired under Napoleon's reign and they were either distributed to other countries or left independent. France was also restored to the rule of Louis XVIII and Spain to the rule Ferdinand VII. The Congress was fairly effective in its goal to maintain the status quo of Europe, and no major wars were fought for over 40 years after.

The Industrial Revolution

A major upheaval in the way people live, work, and think began about 200 years ago and in many ways is still going on today. This change is called the Industrial Revolution, and it accomplished on a massive scale the replacement of human power and animal power with the power of machines. The Industrial Revolution began in England in the 1750s and involved vast changes in the production of goods. These changes included the transition from: handmade goods to machine-made goods; production at home to production in factories (from the domestic system to the factory system); producing small amounts to producing large amounts (mass production); and the increased use of science and new forms of energy (steam power, for example) to speed up production and meet human needs.

Agricultural and Industrial Revolution

What was in effect an agricultural revolution took place by the 17th and 18th centuries. New products like potatoes and maize from the Western Hemisphere and new farming techniques and technologies transformed old peasant agriculture, providing more food for expanding cities and growing numbers of workers who were peasants displaced by new farming methods. Processed products like refined sugar and manufactured textiles became important for the general population.

Agricultural developments in this way further strengthened the commercialization of societies. The industrial revolution, especially in Great Britain and France, transformed the means, methods, and concepts of production and gave immense economic power to those societies that industrialized in this early modern era. By 1800 much of western

Europe no longer comprised basically agricultural societies with growing commercialization. Instead, the profound transformation to industrial societies had begun.

 # Causes of Revolution

The Industrial Revolution began in Great Britain because of a combination of fortunate conditions that existed at the time. First, Britain was fortunate to have large amounts of coal and iron ore. Second, Britain had many good harbors, and coastal and river trade was well developed. Britain also had relatively good roads and numerous canals for the cheap transport of raw materials and finished goods. Third, entrepreneurs and other private individuals had money that they, as capitalists, were willing to invest and risk in business ventures. Fourth, there were large numbers of skilled workers in the population. In addition, there was a great demand for British products, both in the domestic market (within the nation) and in foreign markets.

Given Britain's world dominance, transportation was an advantage that the British enjoyed as well. Britain had a good navy and had built up a shipping industry. Its expanding colonial empire furnished raw materials and markets for goods. Moreover, an agricultural revolution that occurred in the 1700s brought changes in farming that made the Industrial Revolution possible. These changes resulted in the production of more food and required fewer farmers to produce it. Many people left the farms and went to the cities to find work in factories.

Britain had also avoided most of the political calamities that had struck the continent during the eighteenth century. Britain had a stable government that had established a good banking system, promoted scientific experimentation, and passed laws to protect business. Finally, the changes in production came first in the cotton textile industry. Several inventors devised inventions that sped up and improved the manufacture of textiles. These technological changes would eventually be applied to the entire industrializing sector of the British economy.

 # Economic and Social Impact of the Working and Middle Class

The Industrial Revolution fundamentally changed the way people lived. Families moved to industrial cities by the millions to work in the new factories. The first years of adjustment to the new industrial society were a period of severe difficulty for workers. Men, women, and children worked long hours under deplorable conditions in factories.

People were crowded into towns and cities that had made little provision for housing or for sanitation. With more people working in factories and living in cities, occupational, health, and housing problems developed. Moreover, even though they were becoming more populated than rural areas, cities had not gained political power. These problems associated with industrialization developed in Britain as well as in other areas of Europe where industrialization took place.

British Reform Movement

In response to workers' protests and reformers' appeals, various reform measures were adopted. These reforms indicated that Europeans had begun to understand the changes in the working and living conditions of those who labored under the factory system. Reform measures in Britain included social, economic, and political reforms.

Harmful working conditions such as child labor, low wages, faulty ventilation, and dangerous equipment were brought to public attention by the Sadler Report on factories and the Ashley Report on mines. In time, members of Parliament became concerned about children as young as five or six working long hours in factories and mines and about the dangerous, unhealthful conditions for all workers in factories. Laws such as the Factory Act (1833) and the Mines Act (1842) were passed to improve conditions for workers. The need for workers to unite to protect and advance their interests led to the formation of labor unions.

The move to reduce property rights as the basis for suffrage (the right to vote) and to give cities more representation in Parliament led to the passage of the Reform Bill of 1832. This bill also did away with most "rotten boroughs" (areas that no longer had many people but had kept the same amount of representation in Parliament). The middle class, workers, and women were to benefit from the Reform Bill of 1832 and similar legislation passed in the 19th and early 20th centuries. By 1928, for example, Britain provided for universal suffrage. This meant that both women and men had the right to vote. The expansion of suffrage in Britain and other European countries was partially due to changes brought about by the Industrial Revolution.

A succession of other reforms—ranging from factory inspection to the repeal of the hated Corn Laws in 1846—demonstrated that the British political system was flexible enough to cope with the social and economic challenges posed by industrialization. British reform did not extend to universal suffrage, despite the enormous size of the Chartist movement of the 1840s, until 1867. Britain was responsive enough, however, many historians argue, to working-class demands to spare Britain from the wave of revolutionary agitation which swept much of Europe in 1848.

Politican and cultural developments, 1815-1848

The years between 1815-1830 saw the rise of a number of related and competing ideologies, each holding a powerful influence in their own time. That influence often extended well into the future, continuing to the present day.

Liberalism

Beginning in Spain and France during the 1820s, liberalism soon spread to England. Consisting of businessmen and professionals, the liberals wanted modern, efficient self-government, although they were not always for universal male suffrage. They wanted freedom of the press and freedom of the assembly. They wanted constitutions, and Laissez Faire economic policies, such as free trade and low tariffs. They were generally against unions.

Liberalism in the early 19th century is not the same from what we think of as "Liberalism" today. In fact, much of what was liberal in the 19th century (free trade, keeping government out of business) is today considered conservative. Really, liberalism then was the ideology of the bourgeoisie (the business and professional class), and was geared towards protecting bourgeois interests. Still, the liberals invariably argued that what was for their benefit was actually to the benefit of everyone. The liberal tradition of the 19th century has confusingly become what is "conservative" today in the United States.

Conservatism

That relatively confusing transition can perhaps be more clearly understood when one considers that nineteenth-century conservatism advocated support for the monarchy and traditional institutions. Championed by Edmund Burke, who had been horrified by the French Revolution, conservatism argued for prudent and gradual change to be made as slowly as possible.

Nationalism

The Austrian leader, Count Metternich, opposed the French Revolution ideas of freedom and equality. He sought to maintain what had been the status quo prior to the French Revolution. During the Metternich age (1815–1848), there were challenges to the status quo. Nonetheless, most attempts by European peoples against these reactionary policies in order to achieve national unity were put down by force. These attempts, which led to revolutions in 1830 and in 1848, were inspired by a nationalistic spirit, whereby a group of people, such as the Italians, Poles, or Germans, sought to create their own nation and establish self-government. Although most of these revolutions failed, two successful attempts were made in Belgium and Greece in 1830. The Quadruple Alliance, representing the four powers that had defeated Napoleon, did not want these revolutionary movements to succeed. From this alliance emerged the Concert of Europe. This was a form of international government, arranged by concert, or agreement, among its members.

It wanted to keep the balance of power that the Congress of Vienna had set up. Although the Congress could not suppress nationalism permanently, it was able to postpone its success for a half century. The unification of Italy and of Germany in the later 1800s were the first breaks in the territorial settlements of 1815.

Thus, the spirit of nationalism influenced the political history of Europe from 1815 to 1914. Nationalism is the belief that a group of people who share a common culture, language, and historical tradition should have their own nation in a specific area of land. Once the people accomplish their nationalistic goals and form a nation-state, they can then make their own laws and are said to be sovereign and to have autonomy. Nationalism was the guiding force that led to the unification of both Italy and Germany in the late 19th century. The Italians, Poles, Hungarians, Turks, and others who were ruled by the large dynastic states that dominated Europe—the Austrian Empire, the Russian Empire, and the Ottoman Empire—all struggled to win freedom and form their own nation-states.

Socialism

Political scientists and philosophers struggled with the problems presented by industrialization, seeking to discover how the political system should respond. One of these solutions was socialism, which was a criticism of capitalism and called for a basic change in the economic system in order to correct these problems. Socialists maintained that it was necessary to transfer ownership of the means of production (factories, mines, railroads, land) from private individuals to the state.

According to socialist theory, the government, as elected by the people, should own all the means of production and should also make all the key economic decisions. These decisions included: What should be produced? Who should produce it? What should the price be? How should the product be distributed?

This kind of planned, or command, economy is in contrast to a free-enterprise or market economy. In a market economy, according to capitalist principles, the key economic decisions are basically made by private individuals acting on their own. One group of socialists wanted to create an ideal society, or a utopia. Utopian socialists believed that a socialist society would emerge peacefully and that even capitalists would be willing to help create it. Among the utopian socialists of the 19th century were a wealthy British manufacturer, Robert Owen, and a French philosopher, Charles Fourier.

In contrast to utopian socialists were those people who believed in a radically different type of socialism called scientific socialism or communism. That was a type of socialism based on what they believed were scientific ideas about the way society operates. The leading scientific socialist thinkers were Karl Marx and Friedrich Engels of Germany. Their ideas were contained in two books: The Communist Manifesto (1848) and Das Kapital (1867). Their major ideas came to be known as Marxism. Marx and Engels argued that all history is determined by economic conditions. In other words, whichever group or class controls the means of production will control the government. In addition, they argued that in all societies throughout history, there have been struggles for power between two economic groups—the haves and the have-nots. In industrial societies the struggle has taken place between the capitalists, or bourgeoisie, and the workers, or proletariat.

Marx also wrote about surplus value theory. Surplus value was the difference between the price of a good and the wage paid to a worker. According to Marx, this difference was kept by the capitalists as their profit. For Marx, this was wrong, especially because he believed that workers were paid far too little in wages. Such abuse, or exploitation of workers, was unjust.

Finally, Marx and Engels contended that socialism was inevitable. Eventually all of these conditions would lead to depressions and poverty and would result in a violent overthrow by the workers of the government, primarily because the capitalists would not peacefully give up their economic and political power. This communist revolution would result in a dictatorship of the proletariat, a government that would be more just and would rule on behalf of the working class. The government would operate under the theory of socialism. Eventually, a classless society would emerge, and there would be no need for a government; the government would wither away.

The Revolutions of 1830 and 1848

Metternich's reactionary Congress System began to fail in the late 1820s and the early 1830s. In France, the reactionary Charles X had reigned since assuming the throne in 1824. Charles X's reactionary policies antagonized much of the French population, who were used to liberal and republican reforms. The bourgeoisie and radical republicans from the lower classes quickly took to the streets of Paris in the July Revolution, rioting and setting up barricades to stop the military and end traffic and commerce. Charles X quickly abdicated, and the bourgeois leaders of the rebellion moved quickly to install a constitutional monarchy. The revolutionary leaders brought in the Duke of Orleans, known as Louis Philippe. He accepted constitutional monarchy and the principle of the July Revolution, and even changed the official flag of France to the Republican tricolor.

The July Revolution rippled through Europe, starting revolutions in Belgium and Poland. Belgium's revolution was essentially successful. The country ended up with self-government as long as it remained a neutral state, and the other powers agreed not to invade it. Polish nationalists, looking to the successful revolutions in Belgium in France, also decided to revolt in 1830. Czar Nicholas quickly crushed the Polish rebellion.

Spurred by the July Revolution in France, 1830 became a year of revolt. For the most part, however, those revolts resulted in little direct change. Though the revolution in France deposed a king, it also installed a new king: the revolution simply prevented the rights of the bourgeoisie from being trampled by Charles X. Once the revolutions were in motion, however, the powers that be did often have the strength to put them down. Russia had no problem crushing the Polish rebellion. Yet Russia's success stemmed in large part from the domestic factors limiting Britain and France from using the Polish rebellion as a lever to hurt the power of the Russians. Britain was facing its own reform movement, and Louis Philippe did not want to appear to have Napoleonic ambitions. In other words, of the conservative powers, only Metternich and Austria refused to intercede against the Russians on ideological grounds. Britain and France, had they been able, might very well have placed the contingencies of politics above the demands of conservative dogma.

Surprisingly, it was in Britain, where no revolt happened, that the most change occurred. In large part this change resulted from the societal transformation created by the Industrial Revolution. Even so, the July Revolution certainly spurred the political process. The French July Revolution showed the British bourgeoisie that if there was a revolution by the lower classes, the bourgeoisie could quickly assume control and use a working-class revolution to middle-class advantage. The realization that the bourgeoisie was acquiring more and more power and could use that power to create a revolt led the Tory party to grant some concessions.

The British Reform Bill of 1832 was really a compromise, since the reformers did not get everything they wanted. However, the bill was very important in that it made way for future reforms. Especially since the manufacturing cities of the North finally had substantial representation, the balance of power in British politics changed. Wealthy businessmen became part of the political elite. Parties reorganized, and the Whigs, a few radical Tories, and the radical industrialists formed the Liberal Party, while most of the Tories formed the Conservative Party. Under this new political configuration, and with the certain progression of the industrial revolution, further reforms were destined to take place.

By 1848 in France, Louis Philippe's government remained a bourgeoisie-dominated affair, disappointing to the workers who had manned the barricades in 1830. Only a thirtieth of adult males could vote, and Louis Philippe staunchly opposed enlarging the voting base. Popular discontent finally resulted in the February Revolution of 1848. The working classes again put barricades up in the streets, and an unruly Paris mob frightened Louis Philippe into abdicating. The Radical Republicans then managed to get the provisional government to pass socialist programs. This included the creation of National Workshops, which were centralized, state-owned manufacturing establishments where workers would be guaranteed work. In the National Workshops, however, there wasn't any real work for the workers to do, since the government did not take their establishment very seriously. The National Workshops, promising employment, soon became jam- packed with thousands of discontented workers, fermenting still more agitation. In May, the military turned against the lower class agitators. In late June, three days of especially violent class warfare broke out in Paris. The army soon restored order, but the political landscape had changed.

After June 1848, the French began to draw up a new constitution. The constitution included provisions for a strong president, who would be elected via universal male suffrage (all adult males would vote). Four candidates entered the election, which was the first election most of the uneducated, newly enfranchised voters had ever experienced as active participants. The most ambiguous candidate was Louis Napoleon Bonaparte, Napoleon I's nephew. He had no real platform, and few knew his leanings. He merely said that his uncle, Napoleon, had been liberal, and that he would be liberal. Since the name Bonaparte still resonated so strongly among the general population of France, Louis Napoleon won the election over the other, more experienced candidates.

Though claiming to be liberal, the newly elected president was mostly interested in reestablishing order. After gaining support by promising universal male suffrage, he promptly got rid of socialists in the government. He encouraged religious influence in school teaching, and then, after becoming confident of his support base, he declared himself Emperor Napoleon III. The revolution in France ended with a new government, but once again a new dictator.

Like the July Revolution of 1830, the February Revolution of 1848 reverberated throughout Europe, resulting in a series of revolutions, most powerfully in Germany and Vienna. In Britain, the French upheaval revived the Chartist Movement. In London, however, no barricades went up in London's streets. Instead, a new petition went to Parliament.

Vienna, the capital of the ethnically diverse Austrian Empire, was a leading cultural center in Europe. Full of artists, composers, writers, and intellectuals, Vienna was truly the jewel of the Austrian Empire, and the Austrian empire, led by Metternich, was the paragon of reactionary politics. Yet the various ethnic groups in Austria had become increasingly nationalist over the preceding decades, and by now they all yearned to express their individual volksgeist and gain independence. Metternich had worked for years to hold the Austrian Empire together, but now, in the wake of the French February Revolution, the ethnic groups vehemently opposed assimilation.

In March 1848, a radical Hungarian Magyar group led by Louis Kossuth began a vocal independence movement. On March 15, Kossuth's Hungary was granted independence under Hapsburg rule. The Czech movement in Bohemia soon received the same status, and Italian states like Milan soon overthrew Austrian occupation. In June 1848, the revolutions in Austria began to run out of steam. After all, it was a non-industrialized country that did not have a well-developed middle class. Their revolution, largely led by intellectuals and students, could not marshal the same amount of popular support as the bourgeoisie in Western Europe. The 1848 revolutions in Austria came to an end, restoring order in the Empire. But rioting had begun in Berlin, as the 1848 revolution fever crossed from Austria into Prussia. Frederick William IV quickly mobilized the disciplined Prussian army to suppress the revolution. However, he surprised everyone by taking a liberal stance and allowing an election to take place to elect a Prussian assembly.

The elected radical revolutionaries wanted to unite Prussia with all of Germany to create a force that could challenge Russia. The Assembly also desired to grant the Polish minorities living in eastern Prussia a right of self-government. Deciding that the experiment in democratic government had gone on long enough, Frederick William IV changed his mind and dissolved the Prussian Assembly.

The 1848 revolutions inspired a similar nationalist movement in Germany proper. In May 1848, a group of German nationalists met at the Frankfurt Assembly. The goals of the assembly included creating a unified Germany that was Liberal and constitutionally governed. The Frankfurt assembly argued over various topics, including the question of who (the Prussian or Austrian ruler?) should rule a unified Germany.

In December of 1848, the Frankfurt Assembly issued the Declaration of the Rights of the German People, based on the Declarations of the Rights of Man in France and the

Declaration of Independence in the United States. Following the Nationalist rather than Enlightenment ideal, this declaration ignored the universal rights of all mankind and simply proclaimed the rights of Germans.

In 1849, the Frankfurt Assembly offered Germany to Frederick William IV. Though he coveted the territory, Frederick William knew that an acceptance would lead to war with Austria and make him into a constitutional monarch, neither of which he desired. He turned the offer down. Thus, all the deliberation of the Frankfurt Assembly resulted in nothing. Germany remained fragmented after 1848, and the small rulers of the various small German states came back to power.

Politics and Diplomacy in the Age of Nationalism, 1850-1914

The spirit of nationalism influenced the political history of Europe from 1850 to 1914. Once the people in a particular location accomplished their nationalistic goals and form a nation-state, they could then make their own laws and become sovereign. Thus, nationalism was the guiding force that led to the unification of both Italy and Germany in the late 19th century. The Italians, Poles, Hungarians, Turks, and others who were ruled by the large dynastic states that dominated Europe—the Austrian Empire, the Russian Empire, and the Ottoman Empire—all struggled to win freedom and form their own nation-states.

The Unification of Italy and Germany

In 1815 there was no nation called Italy; Italy was really a geographic expression. The Italian Peninsula was divided among large and small states, such as the Lombardy province and the kingdom of Sardinia-Piedmont. Austria, which controlled the states in the northern part of the Italian Peninsula, was against any kind of unity. But by 1861 all the Italian states had become unified into a nation. Those most responsible for bringing unification about were Cavour, who was considered the brain of unification, and who was a successful diplomat who got France to help him fight the Austrians. He also expanded the power of Sardinia-Piedmont by adding to it other Italian states. In addition, Mazzini was the soul of unification, and wrote and spoke eloquently about his desires for Italian unity. He was the founder of the Young Italy movement. The sword of unification, Garibaldi, conquered southern Italy and joined it to the state that Cavour had unified under the control of Sardinia-Piedmont in the north. Finally, King Victor

Emmanuel, formerly the King of Sardinia-Piedmont, became the ruler of a united Italy in March 1861.

Likewise, in 1815 there was no nation called Germany. Instead, there were more than 30 independent German states that had their own traditions, laws, and economic regulations. The largest of these states, Prussia, located in northern Germany, led the movement for unification. The chief obstacle to Prussia's leadership was Austria. It sought to dominate German affairs and did not want to see the German states unified. But by 1871, under the leadership of Prussia's chief minister, Otto von Bismarck, Austria's power was weakened and the German states achieved unification.

Following a policy of blood and iron, Bismarck used military means to achieve his goal of German unity under Prussia's leadership. Under this policy, Prussia won victories in the Danish War (1864), the Austro-Prussian War (or Seven Weeks' War, 1866), and the Franco-Prussian War (1870–1871).

The Treaty of Frankfurt was the treaty that ended the Franco-Prussian War on May 10, 1871. The main importance of this treaty was that it signified the unification of Germany into a real power. Prior to this time, Germany had been a conglomeration of states. Through war with Germany, Otto von Bismarck was able to unify the states (the largest of which was his own Prussia). The treaty additionally transferred the provinces Alsace and Lorraine to Germany, and required that France pay five million francs.

As a result of these wars, Prussia was able to gain land, such as Schleswig-Holstein from Denmark and Alsace-Lorraine from France, unite other German states with Prussia, and reduce the influence of Austria in German affairs. King William I of Prussia became the ruler of a united Germany in 1871 and was called emperor, or kaiser.

Austria-Hungary

The creation of Austria-Hungary was made possible by the Ausgleich [compromise] of 1867, a constitutional compromise between Hungarian aspirations for independence and Emperor Francis Joseph's desire for a strong, centralized empire as a source of power after Austria's defeat in the Austro-Prussian War of 1866. The Hungarians gained control of their internal affairs in return for agreeing to a centralized foreign policy and continued union of the Austrian and Hungarian crowns in the Hapsburg ruler.

Russia

The Russian defeat in the Crimean War was a wake-up call to the autocracy. While St. Petersburg could boast that it commanded the largest army in Europe (in numbers), poor roads, antiquated weapons, and low morale prohibited the effective use of that awesome potential power. The defeat proved to the autocracy in charge that Russia had fallen dangerously behind its Western neighbors, making it vulnerable to future attack and invasion.

Why had Russia lost? Looking to Western models and contrasting Russian society to, say, French or Prussian society, one element remained outstanding: the continued existence in Russia of serfdom. Whether out of genuine progressive beliefs or merely a need for an effective conscript army when the next war developed, Alexander II initiated a period of reform in Russia with the February 19, 1861 Emancipation of the serfs.

This "emancipation," however, was barely related to what the peasants themselves were expecting. While the 360-page statute did give them "the status of free rural inhabitants," peasants were still subject to considerable taxes and a passport system to restrict movement throughout the country. In addition, the land settlement was equally as unfulfilling. Not only did freedom from land obligations only come up for termination in 1863, but also those so-called "temporary obligations" could continue until both the peasants and their local landlords came to a mutually agreeable settlement. When and if that moment ever came, the peasants would receive a small portion of the land through government-financed redemption payments to the landlord—a sum the former serfs would have to repay over a forty-nine year period.

Nevertheless, for autocratic Russia under the Romanov dynasty, this was unprecedented reform. Even more striking were the additional reforms that continued until Alexander's death—the so-called Great Reforms.

France

In December 1848, Louis Napoleon, nephew of Napoleon Bonaparte, was elected president of the Second Republic. Most political leaders in Paris at the time considered him a lightweight—easily manipulated, not terribly bright or competent. Louis surprised the entire nation when, on December 2, 1851, he seized power in a coup d'etat and became dictator of France. Exactly one year later, he declared himself Napoleon III and set out to bring France back to its former glory on the Continent in the Second Empire.

On the surface, France under Napoleon III glittered; in terms of specifics, France was the symbol of success in many areas. During Napoleon III's reign, the French economy flourished due to high demand for French goods, a new banking system put France's financial house in order, and a massive program of public works turned Paris into the envy of the entire world. The city was completely redesigned and improved by Baron Georges Haussmann. Haussmann ripped into poor neighborhoods, replacing them with museums, apartments for the bourgeoisie, brownstones, architectural wonders, wide and straight boulevards, etcetera. Paris, previously the most radical and most volatile of European capitals, took a decidedly more conservative bend—policing was easier, the bourgeoisie pushed the workers into the surrounding suburbs, and the rich came in droves to the center.

Socialism and Labor Unions

The last third of the nineteenth century saw the emergence of the masses as a serious political force in national politics. In Britain, the working classes that had given the country the greatest successes in the industrial revolution clamored to be heard by the ruling elite. Eventually, workers threw their support behind the Labour Party, a political party based on trade unions that advocated the creation of the government welfare state. A similar development took place in Germany, where the Social Democratic party emerged as a political force despite the numerous attempts by the ruling elite to destroy its power. In France, the modernized and centralized state that emerged in the Third Republic united the nation and allowed a mass media culture to emerge. The entire population, receiving the same information and the same interpretation of the news, was galvanized by various events, such as the Dreyfus Affair, which cut right to the heart of French society.

This included a series of scandals that occurred in France in the late 19th century but what was the best known was the Dreyfus affair. In 1894 Captain Alfred Dreyfus was convicted of treason for supplying the Germans with information. However, he was never allowed to examine or refute the evidence against him and maintained that he was innocent. It was uncovered two years later that the traitor had in fact been another army major, and that much of the evidence against Dreyfus was in fact forged. However, the army was more concerned with preserving its reputation than righting any wrongs, and decided to pardon the guilty major and cover up their mistake. Information about the cover up was able to spread due to the book *J'accuse* written by Emile Zola, which was meant to criticize the cover up, and general corruption of the government.

In Austria-Hungary, the power of the bourgeoisie, who had identified their interests with those of the aristocracy, began to weaken as the entire outsider population--ethnic minorities, students, radical right-wing groups--began to emerge in Austrian politics in an atmosphere of demagoguery and fantastic politics.

European Diplomacy, 1871-1900

Foreign policy throughout this era was generally dominated by the imperial game. By 1914, nearly the entire continent of Africa was dominated by Europeans. The ancient states of Asia (i.e. China and southeast Asian societies) also generally succumbed to European invasion. Only the Japanese, after years of modernization and westernization, were able to become imperialists themselves and exert their own interests on the Chinese mainland.

By the end of the nineteenth century, the political balance of power that had kept Europe at a moderate level of peace since 1815 began to unravel. With the consolidation of the German Empire, new alliances and new balances had to be formed; however, the new models would not succeed. The balance of power degenerated into the bipolarization of the European world--namely, the separation of alliances into two groups, the Triple Alliance and the Triple Entente. With an arms race developing and the breakdown of peace in the Balkans, Europe was racing toward utter destruction and World War.

 # Economy, Culture and Imperialism, 1850-1914

In addition to nation states, the period from 1850-1914 saw the rise of transformative new ideas, most particularly the ideas of Darwinian Evolution and Marxism. In 1859, Charles Darwin published On the Origin of Species by Means of Natural Selection, introducing what some historians call the "New Science." His argument was simple: life originated and perpetuated itself through a push-and-pull struggle in which the successful forms adapted themselves to changing conditions and survived, while those that did not chance became extinct. Though he never used the word "evolution," the basics of the argument noticeably suffuse the work. Years later, the notion of "social darwinism"—the application of "survival of the fittest" to political and economic arenas—offered a distinctly conservative approach that advocated unregulated capitalism as the natural form of progress. Darwin, however, never intended such an interpretation of his original biological theory.

World Economy of the 19th Century

During the late nineteenth century, an interdependent world economy developed with Europe at its center. Colonies provided necessary raw materials for the advanced industrial production in European factory centers such as London, Manchester, and Berlin. Capital flowed out of the wealthy nations of Western Europe and into colonial areas to support projects that required heavy capital investment and promised strong returns, such as railroad construction, and industrial development. London became the financial center of the world, serving as a clearing-house for billions of dollars worth of worldwide investment. Capital became fluid throughout the world, loans were extended for the long run, domestic stock markets skyrocketed and, depending upon the extent of empire, remained somewhat insulated from the boom and bust cycles of late nineteenth century capitalism.

Imperialism in Africa and Asia

Historians generally agree that the Scramble for Africa, the rushed imperial conquest of the Africa by the major powers of Europe, began with King Leopold II of Belgium. After reading a report in early 1876 that the rich mineral resources of the Congo Basin (the modern-day Republic of the Congo) could return an entrepreneurial capitalist a substantial profit, the Belgian king ordered the creation of the International African Association, under his personal direction, to assume control over the Congo Basin region. When Leopold asked for international recognition of his personal property in the Congo, Europe gathered at the Berlin Conference, called to create policy on imperial claims. The conference, after much political wrangling, gave the territory to Leopold as the Congo Free State. The conference further decreed that for future imperialist claims to garner international recognition, "effective occupation" would be required. In other words, no longer did plunging a flag into the ground mean that land was occupied. The conference also created some definition for "effective occupation," noting that significant "economic development" was required.

Given notice by King Leopold, the major European powers sprung into action. Within forty years, by 1914 and the end of the scramble for Africa, Great Britain dominated the breadth of the African continent from Egypt to South Africa, as well as Nigeria and the Gold Coast; the French occupied vast expanses of west Africa; the Germans boasted control over modern-day Tanzania and Namibia; the Portuguese exerted full control over Angola and Mozambique. Only Ethiopia and the African-American state of Liberia remained independent. Conquest was relatively easy for the European states: because of previous agreements not to sell modern weapons to Africans in potential colonial areas, Europe easily held the technological and armament advantage. Bands of just a few hundred men and barely a handful of machine guns could obliterate thousands of Africans in mere hours.

The only notable exception to this was Ethiopia, a strategically (especially after the opening of the Suez Canal) placed state at the horn of Africa. By the early 1870s, Ethiopia was in danger of invasion from the British, French, and Italians. With Britain occupying Egypt in 1882, France taking Djibouti in 1884, and Italy dominating Eritrea in 1885, Ethiopia's Emperor Menelik II hatched a daring plan: he would exploit European rivalries and competing interests for the benefit of his country by playing one European power against the other to obtain the modern weapons he needed to protect the boundaries of his state. After Menelik II gave minor concessions to France in return for weapons, Italy grew nervous of the growing French interest in the country and offered Menelik Italian weapons, as well. Soon, Britain and even Russia joined in the game. Throughout the 1880s, Ethiopia grew stronger and stronger as the scramble for Africa went on around it. However, by the early 1890s, Menelik's plans began to unravel as war seemed imminent. In 1889, Italy claimed Ethiopia as an Italian protectorate. When Menelik objected, Italy moved against the emperor all of Europe had armed for over a decade. Italy, longing for a glorious victory to enhance its prestige, ordered its troops into battle. Outnumbered and outequipped, the Italians lost over eight thousand men in the Battle of Adowa on 1 March 1896. Ethiopia remained independent.

Europe's scramble for Africa did not leave South and East Asia at peace. Beginning in the seventeenth century, Great Britain formed and maintained an economic relationship with India. By the end of the eighteenth century, British rule of India was firmly planted and London came to view India as the jewel of its empire. This view guided its foreign policy. For decades, Britain used its military victories and naval superiority to ensure uninterrupted routes to India and beyond, hence its island holdings in the Mediterranean, along the west African coast, at the southern tip of Africa, and, most importantly, the Suez Canal. By the end of the eighteenth century, Indo-British economic ties were so entrenched in a neo-mercantile system that India provided a stepping stone for British trade with China. Britain traded English wool and Indian cotton for Chinese tea and textiles; however, as Chinese demand slackened, Britain sought other means of attracting trade with China.

By the 1830s, Britain realized it could make up the trade deficit with China by selling Indian opium into the Chinese market, making opium Britain's most profitable and important crop in world markets. Eventually, opium poured into China faster than tea poured into British hands; soon, Chinese merchants, already addicted themselves and buying for an addicted population, paid British opium traders in pure silver.

Concerned with the sharp rise in opium addiction and the associated social costs and rise in criminal acts, the Chinese government, led by the aging Manchu dynasty, took action against the British. In 1839, the Chinese destroyed British opium in the port city of Canton, sparking the Opium Wars of 1839- 1842. Easily dominating the backward Chinese forces, the British expeditionary force blockaded Chinese ports, occupied Shanghai, and took complete control of Canton. The 1842 Treaty of Nanking granted Britain extensive trading and commercial rights in China, marking the first in a series of unequal treaties between China and European imperial powers. By the end of the century, after five wars between China and various European powers, France, Britain, Germany, Japan, and Russia held territorial and commercial advantages in their respective spheres of influence. These spheres of influence comprised territories, ports, shipping lines, rivers, etc., in which one nation held exclusive rights to profits and investment. In 1899, the United States, freshly anointed as an international force by its crushing victory over Spain in the 1898 Spanish-American War, objected to the prevalence of spheres of influence. The US advocated and pushed through a new Open Door Policy, an effectively imperial policy that demanded that all nations be given equal and complete rights to Chinese markets.

In addition, and most irritating to the Chinese, Europeans maintained extraterritoriality inside thousands of Chinese port cities. Extraterritoriality meant that foreigners were exempt from Chinese law enforcement and that, though on Chinese land, they could only be judged and tried by officials of their own nation who generally looked the other way when profit was the goal. The resulting lawlessness on the part of the Europeans, combined with the actuality of European economic, political, and military domination of the Chinese, contributed to a virulent anti-imperial sentiment. In 1900, the Boxer Rebellion saw that sentiment explode into mass social unrest and war. With secret encouragement from the Chinese empress, the Boxers, dedicated to ending foreign exploitation in north China, killed scores of European and seized the large foreign legation in Beijing. Reacting immediately, an international expeditionary force of Japanese, Russian, British, American, German, French, Austrian, and Italian troops put down the revolt and sacked Beijing to protect the interests of their respective countries. Afterward, the European powers propped up a weak central government for their own economic benefit.

Beyond China, European imperialism in Asia remained strong. Britain moved into Hong Kong in 1842, into Burma in 1886, and into Kowloon in 1898. France took direct control over the provinces of Indochina—Annam, Tonkin, and Cochinchina (which together make up modern day Vietnam), Laos, and Cambodia.

The First World War and the Russian Revolution

The Congress of Vienna laid the foundation for a century of peace in Europe, broken only by a few brief and local wars (Franco-Prussian, Russo-Turkish, and Crimean). Beginning about 1870, a series of forces combined to move Europe toward war. These forces included a growing spirit of nationalism, increasingly dangerous colonial conflicts, a complex system of entangling alliances, and a rising tide of militarism. Between 1914 and 1918 war swept across Europe. This war was far more destructive of lives and property than any other previous conflict and was considered the first total war. Civilian populations became targets along with soldiers. Terrifying new weapons were used for the first time.

The Causes of the First World War

Many factors contributed to the start of World War I. All the major European powers shared some blame, although historians disagree on whether one nation was more to blame than the others. One factor was imperialism. The desire to control other areas led to sharp competition and rivalry among nations of Western Europe. Examples include: Britain and Germany in Africa and the Middle East; France and Germany in Morocco; and Austria-Hungary and Russia in the Balkans. As European nations struggled to claim more territories in Africa and Asia, they approached the brink of war several times. In addition, nationalism was key. Strong ties to one's nation and/or ethnic group stirred strong emotions. Many groups of people wanted to be free of the control of other nations. For example, Bosnia-Herzegovina wanted to be free from Austria-Hungary so they could be united with Serbia. Other nationalities in the Balkans also wished to be free of control by Austria or the Ottoman Empire and to create their own nations. The Balkans were called the tinderbox of Europe. Nationalism was also a factor in France's wanting revanche (revenge) against Germany for Germany's taking Alsace-Lorraine after the Franco-Prussian War.

Moreover, a network of alliances and the lack of world peacekeeping machinery contributed to the onset of World War I. Two alliances, the Triple Entente (France, Russia, and Britain) and the Triple Alliance (Germany, Austria-Hungary, and Italy) were formed for defensive purposes, but they soon became two armed camps. At this time no organization existed, such as the United Nations, to foster world peace or to help settle disputes among the major powers. A related issue, militarism, also fostered tensions.. As the alliance system divided Europe into two opposing camps, each nation began to increase its military strength. The growth of armies and navies, as well as the development of weaponry, added to the mood of belligerence (warlike attitude) and a tendency to settle disputes by fighting. Manufacturers of arms increased production, as governments sought to build up their military strength. Economic rivalry between Germany and Britain poisoned relations between the two nations. Germany's growing navy was seen by Britain as a threat to its security.

The spark that set off World War I was the assassination of the Austrian Archduke Francis Ferdinand in June 1914 in the town of Sarajevo. The assassin was a Serbian nationalist, Gavrilo Princip, who wanted to free Bosnia-Herzegovina from the Austro-Hungarian Empire and unite them with Serbia.

Austria, backed up by Germany and glad to receive Germany's blank check, threatened Serbia. This angered Russia, causing it to get its armed forces ready for war. Because of the alliance system, country after country was drawn into the conflict and all the major powers were soon fighting each other. A local, regional crisis thus became the spark of a major war. The war, known as the Great War at first, turned into the most violent European conflict since the Napoleonic Wars, almost 100 years before. With neither side able to win, the armies faced one another from trenches. The war was a stalemate until 1917, when the United States entered the war on the side of the Triple Entente nations, or the Allies (Britain, France, and Russia). This helped to bring victory against the Central Powers (Germany, Austria-Hungary, Italy, and Turkey—a late entrant into the war). The war ended in November 1918, having lasted over four years.

The Economic and Social Impact of the War

The war changed the course of the world's history, causing economic chaos and radical social changes in many countries. Some of the most powerful nations in Europe lost their influence and began to decline. Many monarchs lost their thrones. A communist government came to power in Russia, and the seeds of a second great conflict (World War II) were sown when World War I ended and the peace treaty was drawn up.

The war was very costly to the participants. The losers became debtor nations. Many economic problems arising from the war were partly responsible for the worldwide depression that began in 1929.

By conservative estimates, around 9 million soldiers died in battle—many of them defending entrenched front lines that were so stalemated that they rarely moved even a few yards in either direction. Civilian loss of life totaled an additional 13 million. Epidemics of influenza and other diseases, either induced or exacerbated by the war, raised the death toll by at least an additional 20 million. In total, counting battle casualties, civilian deaths, and victims of disease, the loss of life worldwide surpassed 40 million.

By war's end, the map of Europe began to resemble the one we know today. The German and Austro-Hungarian empires ceased to exist. Much of eastern Europe, in particular, was redivided along ethno-linguistic lines, and Hungary, Poland, Lithuania, Latvia, Estonia, and Finland all became independent countries. Several other nations were awkwardly combined into the countries of Yugoslavia and Czechoslovakia. A major reorganization of the Near and Middle East also took place following the war, establishing the forerunners of the countries we know today as Armenia, Turkey, Syria, Lebanon, Saudi Arabia, and Iraq. In addition, the League of Nations was formed in an effort to secure world peace. The political problems and hatreds that emerged in some nations provided a basis for the rise of dictatorships later in Germany and in Italy.

The Peace Settlements

The Versailles Treaty officially ended World War I. It was drawn up at the Paris Peace Conference by David Lloyd George (Britain), Georges Clemenceau (France), Vittorio Orlando (Italy), and Woodrow Wilson (United States). Notably absent were any representatives from Germany. It forced Germany to accept "war guilt" and stripped Germany and Austria-Hungary of much territory. Germany was also forced to pay huge amounts of money to the victors as reparations. It was prohibited from uniting with Austria and required to limit its armed forces (demilitarization). This diktat (dictated peace), as it was called by Germany, caused much resentment in that country and was later used by Hitler as propaganda in his rise to power in the 1930s. The treaty also created the League of Nations.

The League was one of the Fourteen Points that America's Wilson had asked for in an attempt to prevent future wars. The U.S. Senate refused to ratify (approve) the Versailles Treaty. Therefore, the United States did not become a member of the league. For this reason, as well as the fact that it had no enforcement powers, the league was seen as a weak organization.

The Versailles Treaty which was created at the end of WWI was one of the largest motivations for Hitler, and was significant in his rise to power. Although Germany had received no representation at the conference, the treaty forced them to admit they were guilty, and had a war-guilt clause. This significant war-guilt clause required that Germany, already have deep financial struggles as a result of the war, pay huge reparation payments to other countries. This caused lasting economic difficulties and depression in post war Germany that allowed Hitler to rise to power on a platform of the unfair treatment that Germany had received at the hands of the Allied powers.

burden of being tsar, even with a regent in place. However, on the next day Michael also abdicated, leaving Russia with no tsar at all. Responding to this unexpected turn of events, leading Duma members assumed the role of being the country's provisional government. The provisional government was to serve temporarily, until a Constituent Assembly could be elected later in the year to decide formally on the country's future government.

Although the provisional government was quickly recognized by countries around the world as the legitimate governing body of Russia, the Petrograd Soviet held at least as much power and had significantly greater connections with regional authorities in other parts of the country. The Petrograd Soviet was in essence a metropolitan labor union made up of soldiers and factory workers. By the time of Nicholas II's abdication, it had some 3,000 members and had formed an executive committee to lead it. Dominated by Mensheviks, the group was chaotic in structure and favored far more radical changes than did the provisional government.

Though often at odds, the provisional government and the Petrograd Soviet found themselves cooperating out of necessity. With every major decision, the two groups co-ordinated with each other. One man, an ambitious lawyer named Alexander Kerensky, ended up a member of both groups and acted as a liaison between them. In time he would become the Russian minister of justice, minister of war, and then prime minister of the provisional government.

The February Revolution was largely a spontaneous event. It began in much the same way as had dozens of other mass demonstrations in Russia in previous years and might well have ended in the same manner, if the military had not gotten involved. There was no plan or oversight for the way it happened, and few, if any, dedicated Russian revolutionaries were involved—most, such as Vladimir Lenin, were out of the country. Afterward, many political groups competed for power, but they did so relatively peacefully. The two main groups, the provisional government and the Petrograd Soviet, disagreed completely about the direction that Russia should take, yet they did manage to work with each other. Meanwhile, the various rival political parties also developed cooperative attitudes and worked with one another. The arrival of Lenin in Russia in April 1917, however, immediately changed the situation.

Lenin arrived in Petrograd on the evening of April 3, 1917. His arrival was enthusiastically awaited, and a large crowd greeted him and cheered as he stepped off the train. To their surprise, however, Lenin expressed hostility toward most of them, denouncing both the provisional government and the Petrograd Soviet that had helped to bring about the change of power. Although a limited sense of camaraderie had come about among the various competing parties ever since the February Revolution, Lenin would have nothing to do with this mentality. He considered any who stood outside his own narrow Bolshevik enclave to be his sworn enemies and obstacles to the "natural" flow of history.

Lenin recognized that the current Russian leaders' hesitation to pull the country out of World War I was a weakness that could be exploited. He knew that after four years of massive losses and humiliating defeats, the army was ready to come home and was on the verge of revolting. While other politicians bickered over negotiating smaller war reparations—and even over whether Russia might possibly make territorial gains by staying in the war longer—Lenin demanded that Russia exit the war immediately, even if it meant heavy reparations and a loss of territory. With this position, Lenin received growing support throughout the Russian armed forces, which would ultimately be key to his seizing power. Thus, he launched an aggressive propaganda campaign directed specifically at the Russian troops still serving on the front.

During late August and September, the Bolsheviks enjoyed a sudden growth in strength, following their failures during the summer. On August 31, they finally achieved a majority in the Petrograd Soviet, and on September 5, they won a similar victory in the Moscow Soviet. Lenin, fearing arrest after the events of July, continued to hide in rural areas near the Finnish border. As time went on, he become more and more impatient and began calling urgently for the ouster of the provisional government.

Although Prime Minister Alexander Kerensky's authority was faltering, the provisional government was coming closer to organizing the Constituent Assembly, which would formally establish a republican government in Russia. Elections for the assembly were scheduled for November 12. Lenin knew that once this process started, it would be far more difficult to seize power while still preserving the appearance of legitimacy. If there were to be another revolution, it had to take place before then. By the end of the day on October 25, the Bolsheviks had seized power.

After Lenin's government secured power, one of its first major goals was to get Russia out of World War I. Following his Decree on Peace, Lenin sent out diplomatic notes to all participants in the war, calling for everyone to cease hostilities immediately if they did not want Russia to seek a separate peace. The effort was ignored. Therefore, in November 1917, the new government ordered Russian troops to cease all hostilities on the front. On December 15, Russia signed an armistice with Germany and Austria, pending a formal peace treaty (the treaty was not completed until March 1918). The result was the Brest-Litovsk Treaty. As a result of the treaty, war was ended between Russia and the Central Powers. Russia was forced to surrender a significant amount of land, constituting nearly a quarter of their population and industry.

Russia's exit from the war was very costly, but Lenin was desperate to end the war at any cost, as the Germans were threatening to invade Petrograd. In the peace, Lenin consented to give up most of Russia's territorial gains since the time of Peter the Great.

The lost territories included Finland, Poland, Latvia, Lithuania, Estonia, Ukraine, Belarus, Bessarabia, and the Caucasus region, along with some of the coal-mining lands of southern Russia. The Soviets would not regain these territories until the end of World War II.

After the October Revolution, the Bolsheviks had very little planning in place, and their rule got off to a rough start when they came in behind the SRs in the elections of the Constituent Assembly. The working class was still a minority in Russia; the Bolsheviks would change that in time, but at the outset their rule could be maintained only by force.

The Bolsheviks faced major opposition from within Russia and for many different reasons. Among the most contentious issues was Russia's costly exit from World War I. Though many had wanted out of the war, they did not approve of Lenin's readiness to lose vast amounts of territory. In addition, the Bolsheviks' sudden dismissal of the Constituent Assembly and their silencing of all other political voices was offensive to many as well. The result was the Russian civil war, which would be horrifically painful for the country and that, in the end, would cost even more lives than had World War I. The years following, with the violence of Joseph Stalin's purges and forced collectivization of Russia's lands, would not be much better.

Europe Between the Wars

With the end of World War I, the old international system was torn down, Europe was reorganized, and a new world was born. The European nations that had fought in the Great War emerged economically and socially crippled. Economic depression prevailed in Europe for much of the inter-war period, and debtor nations found it impossible to pay their debts without borrowing even more money, at higher rates, thus worsening the economy to an even greater degree. Germany especially was destroyed economically by World War I and its aftermath: the reparations to Britain and France forced on Germany by the Treaty of Versailles were impossibly high.

The League of Nations represented an effort to break the pattern of traditional power politics, and bring international relations into an open and cooperative forum in the name of peace and stability. However, the League never grew strong enough to make a significant impact on politics, and the goals of deterrence of war and disarmament were left unaccomplished.

The political atmosphere of the inter-war years was sharply divided between those who thought the extreme left could solve Europe's problems, and those who desired leadership from the extreme right. There were very few moderates, and this situation kept the governments of Britain, France, and Eastern Europe in constant turmoil, swinging wildly between one extreme and the next. Extreme viewpoints won out in the form of totalitarian states in Europe during the inter-war years, and communism took hold in the Soviet Union, while fascism controlled Germany, Italy and Spain.

The extremist nature of these disparate ideologies turned European politics into an arena for sharp conflict, erupting in Spain during the late 1930s in the form of the Spanish Civil War, after which Francisco Franco became dictator. In Germany, Adolf Hitler's fascist Nazi Party came to power during the 1930s and prepared once again to make war on Europe. With Britain and France tied up in their own affairs, the path to World War II lay clear.

 # The Great Depression

From 1925 to 1929, Europe entered a period of relative prosperity and stability. However, unemployment remained high, and population growth outstripped economic growth. During this time, world trade increased and speculative investment increased as the result of better economic times. US creditors, flush with capital coming in from Europe, led this speculative movement.

Germany continued to struggle with reparations payments, and in 1930, the Young Plan replaced the Dawes Plan, lowering annual payments yet again, but to no avail. In attempts to maintain benefits for the unemployed and drive prices down, taxes were hiked, and unemployment shot up again. As the Great Depression that had struck the United States in 1929 began to set in throughout Europe in the early 30s, banks began to collapse. Despite international loans, Germany, and Europe as a whole, plunged into depression, during which currencies collapsed and all hope of stability was dashed. Despite efforts to stabilize world prices and European employment, Europe remained mired in depression until the outbreak of World War II.

 # International Politics, 1919-1939

The League of Nations was at first heralded as the bastion of a new system of international relations in Europe. The so-called 'old diplomacy' is known as the Westphalian System, since it had been in place since the Treaty of Westphalia, signed at the end of the Thirty Years War in 1648 by the major European powers. Under the Westphalian system the elites of government often met in secret to determine the fate of Europe and the world. World War I shattered the old system along with the empires that had maintained it. American participation in the war was a major step toward a shift in the balance of world power, and the beginning of the end for European dominance. The brutality, and to some, apparent needlessness, of the war and the changing face of European geography led to new ideas about how international affairs should be managed. The secretive nature of the Westphalian system had led to petty resentments, the pursuit of narrow self-interest, and the division of Europe into warring camps. Many, including Woodrow Wilson, felt that a more open, all- inclusive system would be more fostering to cooperation, a concept of international justice, and peace. The League was seen as a way to institutionalize these goals and strive for peace as a collective world community.

The founding and structure of the League of Nations was established primarily for the purpose of preventing future wars, a new concept for Europeans who traditionally believed that war was a necessary and inevitable outgrowth of international relations. However, the League could not come to a decision on how best to do this, without infringing on the sovereignty of the member countries, as would have been the case if the Treaty of Mutual Assistance or the Geneva Protocol had been passed. The failure of these two measures left the League with only the power to invoke economic sanctions against a nation determined to be the aggressor in a conflict, and greatly called into question the authority and ability of the League to mediate conflicts. The League of Nations thus exercised only limited powers, and did so clumsily. Most powerful nations preferred to manage their affairs outside of the League, only rarely deferring to the League's authority. Despite these shortcomings, the League of Nations did accomplish some of its unification and pacification goals, and perhaps most importantly, set the stage for the United Nations, which would take its place after World War II.

Stalin's Five-Year Plans and Purges

Joseph Stalin's rule in the Soviet Union proved to be one of the most brutal dictatorships in modern history. From his consolidation of complete power in 1929 until his death in 1953, he was responsible for millions of deaths, starting with the elimination of all possible rivals. Stalin created his own secret police, which spied on, arrested, tortured, and executed party members, government officials, artists, writers, clergy, workers, and peasants he suspected of not supporting his policies. In time, his fears became paranoia (fear and suspicion of everyone, often without cause), and even close friends and relatives were killed. From 1935 to 1936 Stalin conducted a series of show trials (hearings where the verdicts were decided in advance) known as the purges, in which hundreds of leading Communists were arrested, forced to confess to crimes they had never committed, and executed.

In 1928, dissatisfied with the slow growth rate of Soviet industry, Stalin abandoned Lenin's agenda in favor of centralized economic planning. Goals for agriculture and industry (often unrealistically high), as well as the means for achieving them, were laid out in a series of Five-Year Plans. These were designed to make the U.S.S.R. catch up with the other industrialized nations by emphasizing the industrial development of steel, iron, coal, and oil.

It consolidated farms and factories from smaller individually owned entities and made them properties of the government. Production goals were set which, although they were entirely unrealistic, workers were under a lot of pressure to meet. Throughout his reign Stalin actually implemented three main five year plans. The first plan focused heavily on transportation systems through which coal, oil and steel could be more effectively transported. During this time Stalin relied heavily on tactics of terrorism and intimidation which caused people to rebel in ways such as killing their farm animals rather than losing them to large farms. The result was declining agricultural production. Workers were treated very poorly, with bad working conditions and low pay. Even had the workers had extra pay it would have done them little use because they would have had no access to consumer goods – there just weren't any produced.

The second five year plan resulted in a tripling of the production of oil, coal and steel which transformed Russia into a world industrial power. The rations on food were removed, though the average working condition remained quite poor. The third five year plan had its focus on the production of weaponry.

Although the plans were effective in the sense that they improved industrialization and military ability, there were unsuccessful in the sense that this was achieved through terrorism of the people. Estimates for the number of people murdered under his reign are around 20 million, if not many more. Throughout his reign Stalin continued to impose quotas and terrorize the people, resulting in the eventual downfall of the Soviet Union.

To end the opposition of peasants to collectivization, Stalin began a series of genocides (mass killings) from 1932 to 1937, claiming that he was eliminating the kulaks (wealthy peasants who supposedly exploited their neighbors). In fact, few of the 14.5 million peasants who died by execution, perished in Siberian labor camps, or starved in Stalin's man-made famine in Ukraine (1932–1933) were kulaks. While outright opposition was finally crushed by these genocides, the peasants did not fully cooperate, and the collectivization program failed to achieve its goal. When World War II interrupted the Third Five-Year Plan in 1941, only heavy industry had made any progress. The loss of life and human suffering that this modest gain had cost was enormous. It is no wonder that many Soviet citizens, especially Ukrainians, first saw the invading German armies as liberators in 1941. When Nazi Germany invaded the U.S.S.R. in 1941, the population was forced once again to resort to the scorched earth.

At the time that all of this was happening in Russia, the beginnings of reform were coming to China as well. In view of the changes in Russia, shortly after the Bolshevik

Revolution brought Lenin to power, the Chinese Communist Party was established, one of the members of which was a man named Mao Zedong. Struggles between various factions within the country, along with war with the Japanese during WWII, allowed the communists seize power and Mao established the People's Republic of China. Mao maintained a strong hold over the country during his rule. A group of radical supporters spread his doctrines throughout China. His support was especially strong in the younger generations whom he heavily recruited. There was no toleration for dissension and many people were bullied, intimidated or terrorized into compliance, in addition to many who were imprisoned for years without proof of wrongdoing. Although he instituted many positive policies, such as supporting population growth (resulting in the population doubling) and encouraging agricultural growth, his severe tactics of execution, imprisonment and torture resulted in the deaths of over 40 million people (with some estimates ranging to nearly twice that number).

Italy and Germany Between the Wars

In 1915, the French, British, and Russians had promised territory to Italy in exchange for joining the Allied cause. However, when the war ended, the principle of national self determination stood in the way of Italian efforts to collect on this promise. Under this widely accepted philosophy, the Allies could not grant Italy the territory it had been promised because it was not theirs to give, since most of the territory promised to Italy was populated by non-Italians. The Italian Prime Minister Vittorio Orlando returned from the Paris Peace Conference at the close of World War I embarrassed and empty-handed, with nothing to show for the sacrifices of the Italian war effort. The Italian people naturally turned against Orlando's government, as well as the returning veterans, and both were widely despised. Veterans were often physically and verbally abused if they appeared publicly in uniform, adding to the misery of returning home from the war to widespread unemployment and poverty.

Like the other warring nations, Italy had borrowed extensively to finance its war effort. In 1919, the Italian national debt was six times its pre-war level, and the lira had depreciated to one-third its pre-war value. To make matters worse, the democratically elected Chamber of Deputies, Italy's primary governing body, was unpaid, and thus prone to corruption and bribery. Amid the chaos of the early inter-war years, Benito Mussolini founded the Fascist Party, the Fascio di Combattimento, in March 1919. The Fascist Party, composed largely of war veterans, was vehemently anti-communist, and advocated the glorification of war, which they claimed displayed the nobility of the Italian soul. The Fascists thought Italy was destined to recapture the glory of Rome.

Mussolini's rule as dictator fell nicely into the established totalitarian mold of an omnipotent state apparatus that controlled thought and suppressed dissent, demanding obedience and uniformity. Mussolini's ascent to power is also a perfect example of the means by which dictators during the inter-war years commonly rose to power, by literally beating the legal state apparatus down through brutality and intimidation until it had no choice but to legally accept the imposed government. Though Mussolini's means of ascension to power were by no means legal, in the end, he was granted control of the government by the king himself. This legitimization of totalitarian government was seen commonly throughout the twentieth century.

Likewise, the rise of Nazi Germany was the capstone of the inter-war period, and led to the outbreak of World War II, shattering the tenuous peace. The Nazi regime's progress was paralleled by the life of its leader, Adolf Hitler. Born in a small town in Austria, Hitler dreamed of being an artist. Unable to demonstrate sufficient artistic skill for entrance into the art academy in Vienna, he did odd jobs and developed an interest in politics. In 1914, Hitler joined the German army, and earned the iron cross for bravery as a message-carrier. He was immensely disturbed by the German defeat in World War I, and blamed the loss on the socialists and Jews, who he said had surrendered the nation.

In 1920, Hitler seized control in the German Workers Party, changing its name to the National Socialist German Workers Party, called the Nazi Party for short. On November 9, 1923, Hitler and World War I hero General Ludendorf attempted a small revolution known as the Beer Hall Putsch. Hitler had jumped onto a beer hall table and proclaimed the current Weimar government overthrown. He and Ludendorf led their supporters into the street, and were promptly arrested. Hitler spent two years in prison, where he wrote *Mein Kampf (My Struggle)*, which outlined his future policies, centered on the theory of Aryan superiority and Jewish inferiority.

Released in 1925, Hitler honed his oratorical skills and worked for the advancement of the Nazi party. Such advancement was slow in coming through the years 1925 to 1929, a fairly stable period in Europe. However, as the world became mired in depression and unemployment rose, so did support for the Nazi Party, which promised employment and a return to glory for the nation. In 1932 the Nazis won 37.3 percent of the popular vote and occupied 230 seats in the German Reichstag. There was little stability in the German government at this time, and seeking a solution to this instability, President Paul von Hindenburg appointed Hitler chancellor on January 30, 1933. Once in office, Hitler dissolved the Reichstag and persuaded Hindenburg to issue a decree granting Hitler authority to prohibit public meetings, the wearing of political uniforms, and publication of dissenting opinions.

On February 27, 1933, the Reichstag building burned down and a retarded Dutch boy claiming he worked for the communists was arrested for arson. There is evidence to prove that the Nazis themselves had set the fire, but in any case, Hitler used the incident to persuade Hindenburg to restrict all individual rights and declare that the central government could oust any state government failing to maintain order. Hitler systematically took control of all of the state governments this way. Hitler's private army, the S.A., roamed the streets terrorizing political opponents. Even so, the Nazis only won 43.9 percent of the vote in 1933. To gain a two-thirds majority Hitler formed an alliance with the Nationalist party, and declared the communist party illegal.

On March 23, 1933, the Reichstag passed the Enabling Act, giving Hitler the power to make decrees with the status of law, and ending elections. When Hindenburg died in 1934, Hitler fused the positions of chancellor and president into one office: 'Der Fuhrer.' He took control as dictator. Hitler constructed the Third Reich under his dictatorship, using the Gestapo, the secret police, to stifle all dissent.

Hitler's vague policy included a planned economy in which the unemployed were put to work on government projects, working hours were shortened to open up jobs, and labor was forbidden to organize. The government oversaw all functions of the economy. All education and speech was controlled. Curricula and textbooks were rewritten to reflect Nazi ideology, and all movies, newspapers, radio, and art were regulated by the vigilant Ministry of Propaganda, under Joseph Goebbels. One of the Ministry's main tasks was to mobilize German anti- Semitism in support of Nazi persecution of German Jews, which would reach its climax in the Holocaust, begun in earnest in 1941. The persecution of the Jews was a major step in Hitler's plan to conquer all of Europe for the Aryan race, a plan that resulted in the outbreak of World War II.

The Second World War and Contemporary Europe

Although World War II started in Europe, it soon became a global conflict that dwarfed all previous wars in geographical extent and in human and material losses suffered. Fighting took place on three continents—Europe, Africa, and Asia—and on the seas, lands, and oceans around the globe. More nations (over 50) were belligerents (fighters in the war) than in any war in history. The chief antagonists on the Allied side were Great Britain, France, the United States, the Soviet Union, and China. On the opposing side were Germany, Italy, and Japan, the so-called Axis powers.

The Causes and the Course of the Second World War

Many of the causes of World War II were similar to those that brought on the first world war. After World War I, many nations hoped to prevent another war by establishing what could be called a house of peace. The foundations of this house included: the Versailles Treaty, the League of Nations, disarmament conferences (held in Washington, D.C., and in London), and the Kellogg-Briand Pact, which attempted to outlaw war. Unfortunately, the house of peace crumbled for a number of reasons, most of them due to the actions of the Axis powers (Germany, Italy, and Japan). The basic causes of the war similar to those of World War I. First, militarism was crucial. Large amounts of money were spent on weapons, and military strength was seen as a source of national pride. The leaders of the Axis nations were always seen in military dress.

Second, nationalism and racism were key. The Axis nations saw themselves as superior to others and with the right therefore to extend their culture and their borders (the German master race" theory, the Italian wish to revive the ancient Roman Empire, the Japanese pride based on Shinto teachings and the necessity to establish a new order in Asia). Those factors converged with imperialism. The Axis nations sought to take over other lands for political, racist, and economic reasons. Japan moved into China (1931, 1937); Italy conquered Ethiopia (1938); and Germany annexed Austria (the Anschluss, or union) and Czechoslovakia (1938, 1939).

Finally, diplomacy failed. The democratic nations of Europe and the United States did little to curb the aggressive policies of Germany, Italy, and Japan. The League of Nations condemned some of these aggressive moves but was unable to take any other action. The long-held policy of appeasement compounded these problems. To give in to a potential aggressor, hoping that the aggressor will be content and not commit any further harmful acts is called appeasement. It later came to mean the policy of accepting territorial aggression against small nations in the hope of avoiding a general war. This policy was followed by the British prime minister, Neville Chamberlain, at the Munich Conference in 1938. There, he agreed to accept German annexation of the Sudetenland portion of Czechoslovakia in return for Hitler's guarantee of independence for the rest of Czechoslovakia. The policy proved to be a failure when Hitler later sent the German army to occupy all of Czechoslovakia in violation of the Munich Agreement.

The German attack on Poland in September 1939 was the actual start of the war. Britain and France finally realized that they would have to use military force to stop Hitler's aggression and threat to conquer all of Europe. Just prior to its attack on Poland, Germany signed a nonaggression pact with the Soviet Union. Under this agreement, Russia would take over eastern Poland and the Baltic states of Estonia, Latvia, and Lithuania and would not contest Hitler's attempt to take over western Poland. Also, Russia and Germany promised not to fight each other.

Using blitzkreig warfare ("lightning war"), Germany overran most of Europe, except for England, by 1941. In June of that year, Germany broke its promise not to attack Russia and invaded that nation. The Russians suffered great losses and were driven back to the outskirts of Moscow, Leningrad, and the Volga River, where they held and gradually began to turn the tide. Also, in 1941 the United States entered the war after its navy was attacked by Japan at Pearl Harbor, Hawaii. The nations now fighting the Axis powers were known as the Allies (United States, Britain, France, Soviet Union). With the invasion of Normandy in western France on June 6, 1944 ("D-Day"), Allied forces began to retake German-held lands and pushed the Germans eastward. Russian forces entered the German-held Eastern European nations and pushed the Germans westward. On May 8, 1945 ("V-E Day"), Germany surrendered. In Asia, by 1941 Japan had conquered large areas of East and Southeast Asia. These Pacific areas were slowly retaken by U.S. forces between 1942 and 1945. In August 1945 the United States dropped two atomic bombs on the Japanese cities of Hiroshima and Nagasaki. On September 2, 1945 ("V-J Day"), Japan surrendered.

One major development of the war, the Holocaust, remains one of the most tragic in human history. This word refers to the intentional persecution and systematic murder of European Jews by the Germans from 1933 to 1945. Six million Jews were exterminated, mostly in concentration camps such as Auschwitz, Dachau, and Treblinka. The planned extermination of a group of people because of their religion, race, or ethnicity is called genocide. The genocidal tactics of the Nazis were a horrible extension of Hitler's anti-Semitic attitudes. The world stood by and did nothing while these tactics such as gas chambers, ovens, and firing squads were being used. There were scattered instances of Jewish armed resistance, such as in the Warsaw Ghetto Uprising in 1943. After the war, at the Nuremberg War Crimes Trials, several Nazis were found guilty of genocide and of crimes against humanity. In addition to Jews, other groups of people labeled "inferior" by the Nazis were also sent to the concentration camps. These included homosexuals, Jehovah's Witnesses, Gypsies, Slavs, and mentally retarded people.

Postwar Europe

The world of 1945 bore little resemblance to the world of the 1930s. Europe was shattered and lay in ruins, its people facing an uncertain future. Years of fighting had resulted in decimated infrastructure, communication and agriculture, in addition to the many lives which had been lost. As a result, many countries were turning to communism. In an attempt to stop the spread of communism through Western Europe, the

Marshall Plan (officially called the European Recovery Plan) was created. The plan offered financial aid to Western European countries, and over the course of a few years nearly 13 billion dollars worth of aid, in the form of both cash and supplies, was distributed. This allowed European economies to grow at unprecedented rates.

The United States and the Soviet Union became the two leading superpowers and eventually clashed on many issues in what became known as the Cold War. Germany was divided into four zones of occupation—American, British, French, and Soviet. Poland's boundaries with the Soviet Union were changed, moving further westward. The Soviets established a sphere of influence, as an imperialist power, in many Eastern European nations. Some Soviet activities were in violation of the Yalta agreements of 1945. Britain and France lost some of their status as world powers; nationalistic movements in their colonies were to lead to a loss of their empires. The Allies helped to create the United Nations.

The Korean War is considered to be the first armed conflict of the Cold War. At the end of World War II the country had been divided into northern and southern portions. North Korea was communist, and South Korea remained a republic under US occupation. However the situation between the two portions of the country was strained and soon North Korean forces began invasions into the South. The United States acted quickly, sending many of its own troops and requesting and receiving aid from the newly established United Nations. The Truman Doctrine was invoked in support of this action. With both portions of Korea being supported by much stronger powers, the war was really a product of the Cold War.

The Truman Doctrine evolved from a speech that President Truman gave to Congress requesting that four million dollars and military aid be given to Greece. The reason for this was the fact that if Greece did not gain stability it would "fall" to communism. He urged the protection of "free peoples who are resisting attempted subjugation by armed minorities or by outside pressures" (by which he was referring to communism). The Truman Doctrine is the position that the United States held through the Cold War- that the United States would work to combat the spread of communism by giving aid to countries in need. This policy became known as containment.

The Truman Doctrine contrasts with the Brezhnev Doctrine which was issued many years later. The Brezhnev Doctrine was a statement issued by USSR leader Leonid Brezhnev and stated that once a country had become communist, it would stay that way forever. It stated that the countries had a responsibility to each other, and that the USSR had the right to use military force to ensure that countries remained communist.

The main difference between these two documents is that the Truman doctrine was proactive and stated that the United States would work to keep additional countries from converting to Communism. The Brezhnev Doctrine, on the other hand, focused on maintaining those countries which already had converted to communism.

The first policy which the Truman Doctrine was used to support was giving financial and military aid to the Greek monarchy during a civil war in the late 1940s. When the Greek Civil War weakened the country and threatened to result in its conversion to communism, President Truman requested that Congress grant them financial and military aid. Approximately 400 million dollars worth of aid was sent to Greece (though no military were sent), allowing the monarchy to maintain control of the country. This was effectively the first anti-communist action taken by the United States.

The cold war proved to be the most costly ever fought. The loss of life and property in World War II far surpassed that of any previous conflict. The economies of many European nations were destroyed. Communism spread into the nations of Eastern Europe.

In addition, more people, soldiers and civilians, were killed than in any other war. Much of this was due to new highly destructive weapons, as well as to the racist policies of the Axis powers. At war's end, millions of people had become refugees and displaced persons.

The period after World War II (the postwar period) was marked by the dominance of two superpowers—the United States and the former Soviet Union. Each nation had different philosophies about politics, economics, and human rights. Each thought it was superior to the other. The two nations engaged in a "cold war," which was not a shooting war but a war of words and propaganda; it also involved competition in science, weapons, and seeking friends among the new emerging nations in Africa and Asia. Western European nations sided with the United States in what was called the free world. The Soviet Union occupied the Eastern European nations and, with them, formed the communist bloc.

When Mikhail Gorbachev came to power as head of state of the Soviet Union, one of the programs that he implemented was Perestroika, an economic restructuring. Essentially, the program brought about a sort of democratization of the economy. The control of the government over the market was reduced and people were allowed more freedom in decision making. He also moved resources from maintaining the military to helping provide for the basic necessities of citizens. Gorbachev hoped to revitalize the Soviet economy by changing the people's attitude about working. He instituted better working conditions and attempted to increase leisure time.

As the 1990s began, however, the Cold War came to an end, seen in the peaceful overthrow of communist governments in Eastern European nations such as Poland and Czechoslovakia. But the most striking event marking the end of the Cold War and the decline of communism occurred on December 8, 1991, when the leaders of Russia and other Soviet republics announced that the Soviet Union no longer existed. Taking its place would be several independent nations, for example, Russia, Ukraine, and Belarus, that would be members of the Commonwealth of Independent States. The Cold War era, from 1945 to 1991, was distinguished by certain key events in Western Europe.

As a result of the division of Europe, a cold war (political, economic, and diplomatic conflict without open military conflict) developed. In 1949 the countries of Western Europe and the United States formed a military alliance, NATO (North Atlantic Treaty Organization), in response to Stalin's takeover of Eastern Europe and his unsuccessful attempts to install communist governments in Greece, Turkey, and Iran. This policy, called containment (to limit the spread of communism to areas where it already existed), was answered by the U.S.S.R. with the creation of the Warsaw Pact, an alliance of the Soviet Union and the Eastern bloc or communist satellite countries. The military buildup that resulted from the Cold War put an even greater strain on the Soviet economy, which was still suffering from the devastation of World War II. The U.S.S.R.'s new superpower status was expensive to maintain, and Soviet consumers bore the burden.

With the death of Stalin, there was a period of readjustment from the fear and suffering the Soviet dictator's rule had brought. This great thaw from Stalinism (1953–1958) allowed some freedom of political and cultural expression (mostly denouncing Stalin). However, this was short-lived. When Nikita Khrushchëv (1958–1964) took power as first secretary and premier, these freedoms ended. Khrushchëv attempted to increase industrial and agricultural production through a series of plans, particularly productivity incentives and an expansion of agricultural development into thinly populated areas (virgin lands program). Khrushchëv's policies failed due to the inefficiency of the bureaucratic Soviet system, the lack of incentives to produce in the factories, and the severe forces of nature in Russia. Many conservatives from the Stalinist period resented Khrushchëv. They used his setback in the Cuban missile crisis and the failures of his economic reforms to oust him from power in 1964.

Khrushchëv was succeeded by Leonid Brezhnev (1964–1982), who, unlike Stalin or Khrushchëv, did not have complete power and was answerable to top Communist Party officials. Despite the great need for change that had prompted Khrushchëv's programs, Brezhnev feared that reform would undermine the authority of the Communist Party. The policy of concentrating on heavy industry was therefore continued, except for one unsuccessful experiment to expand consumer goods production in the Ninth Five-Year Plan (1971–1975). By 1972 the antagonism between the Soviet Union and Communist China and the fear produced by improved relations between China and the United States forced Brezhnev to adopt a policy of détente (understanding) with the United States and Western Europe.

This first thaw in the Cold War also resulted in the first of two SALT (Strategic Arms Limitation Talks) agreements, in which both NATO and the Warsaw Pact nations agreed to restrict the development of antiballistic missile systems. These were followed by START (Strategic Arms Reduction Talks) in the Gorbachëv era. Despite détente, Brezhnev continued to suppress dissent and oppose any domestic reform.

Science, Philosophy, the Arts and Religion

The Scientific Revolution describes the evolution of scientific understanding throughout the course of history. Generally considered to be the first monumental event of the scientific revolution is the proposal of the Heliocentric model (sun centered model) of the solar system by Nicolas Copernicus. All previous models of the solar system had the faults of being inconsistent or overly complex. Copernicus was challenging centuries of acknowledged experts and beliefs by presenting his theory. It challenged both Ptolemy's geocentric model and Aristotle's claim of uniform circular motion of the planets. A second important figure of the Scientific Revolution was Galileo. Galileo worked to build upon Copernicus' theories by developing mathematical methods to support the science behind them. An important element of Galileo's studies was the telescope. Galileo is famed for his invention of the telescope and he was the first to use one to study the universe. Galileo also studied motion and kinematics extensively.

Following Galileo, Sir Isaac Newton furthered the extent of knowledge through his studies of motion. Sir Isaac Newton was a famous scientist and mathematician who lived during the Enlightenment. What he is most known for is his study of gravitation his three laws of motion, namely, the principle of inertia, the relationship between force and acceleration, and the idea of equal and opposite reactions. Along with his scientific discoveries, Newton is also known for his work in the field of calculus. Much of his scientific work was proved through his development of mathematical laws to demonstrate it. Newton created mathematical models to describe forces, gravitation, objects in free fall, uniform motion and others.

Blaise Pascal was one of the great minds of the seventeenth century. Among his many inventions is the one of the first mechanical calculators. Also, from his study of pressure came the invention of the syringe. He also studied probability extensively and developed the law of probability. Pascal was also deeply religious and one of his most famous philosophies is referred to as Pascal's Wager. This is Pascal's argument in favor of religion on the basis that, because the existence of God cannot be proved or disproved, it is wiser to follow religious practices because little is lost by it in the long run if in the end God does not exist. On the other hand, a person stands to lose a lot if they do not follow religious practices and in the end God does exist.

The "post-Industrial Revolution" refers to changes that have taken place in this century. These changes took place in such fields as the gathering of information technology, communications, and the manufacture of products. These changes have accelerated contact and diffusion among culture regions and promoted global independence. This has, in turn, widened the impact of machines and medical technology on the lifestyles, work patterns, and standard of living of people in all societies.

Historical consumption patterns look little like those practiced today. Considering life just two or three centuries ago would reveal a world in which the vast majority of individuals worked long hours in agricultural settings and purchased few or no consumer goods. A large part of the change in consumption patterns can be traced to the Industrial Revolution, after which goods became available at increasingly low prices and in greater amounts. The transformation to more consumption oriented patterns is referred to as the birth of a consumer society.

Computers have been the key to the changes of the post-Industrial Revolution. The tiny low-cost silicon chip has brought the most important change in human communications since the printing press. A silicon chip makes it possible to perform millions of calculations in a second and to store vast amounts of information. Today's largest computers can perform as many as 800 million calculations a second and store 4 million words. These stored data can be retrieved instantly and transmitted to any location on earth or even into space. Computers today are used in many areas of human activity. These include: international financial and banking transactions and investments; automation of industrial production and product distribution; informational data analysis, sharing, storage, and retrieval; news gathering and spreading via electronic telecommunication; and weapons development, monitoring, and control.

The advances in medical technology over the past century have prolonged human life and increased its quality. Vaccinations have helped make humans immune to many deadly diseases, while new treatment techniques have increased survival rates for many others. Likewise, improved treatment of wounds and injuries, as well as organ transplants and artificial body parts, have enabled people to live full lives where in the past they might have been severely disabled.

Attitudes have also changed. People are seen as "physically challenged" rather than handicapped and are encouraged to strive to reach their potential. Accessible public facilities and special activities and support groups have helped to enrich the lives of those with physical disabilities.

Preventing diseases has also become an important medical concern. Scientists have researched the effects of most human activities from smoking to jogging, from eating red meat to living near nuclear power plants. Although there is not always agreement on the implications of such studies, the information does provide people with knowledge and possible choices. Biotechnology and genetic engineering hold both a promise and a threat for the future. The development of new organisms (biotechnology) may help control diseases or pollutants, but long-term effects may be hard to predict. And the capacity to alter human genes (genetic engineering) that control a person's individual makeup raises ethical as well as medical issues. Underlying all this is the issue of cost. Medical treatment grows ever more expensive, even in developed nations. In the developing nations, it is one more factor that must be considered in making decisions regarding use of limited financial resources.

Deism is a religious belief which affirms the existence of God. Stated most simply, deists argue that because all things exist, there must have been a creator. However, deism also argues that this God does not intervene in the universe. Rather, they support the idea of a watchmaker God – that God created the universe and now simply lets it run its course without intervention. Because of this, deists tend to reject the idea of the Bible, miracles and prophecies. Many of the founding fathers of the United States were in fact deist, such as a Benjamin Franklin, Thomas Jefferson, Thomas Paine, James Madison and Alexander Hamilton. In addition, many other important historical figures were deist such as Sir Isaac Newton, Voltaire and John Locke.

Denis Diderot was a French philosopher and writer during the Enlightenment. He is most famous for his work, *Encyclopedie*. Diderot looked critically upon the Catholic Church, noting their historical tendency to destroy books and free thinkers. *Encyclopedie* was meant to combat this policy by containing a record of everything that was known, and thereby preserve the information. Diderot believed that all people had the right to educate themselves further. The first volume was published in 1751 and was followed over the years with 27 additional volumes. Although the French government initially attempted to ban the books, it became impossible due to their popularity.

Date	*Invention*	*Inventor*	*Description*
1450	Printing Press	Johannes Gutenberg	Revolutionized printing press allowing literacy and books to spread
1593	Thermometer	Galileo Galilei	Consisted of water in a glass bulb

Date	Invention	Inventor	Description
1609	Telescope	Galileo Galilei	Galileo was the first to use a telescope in observing the night sky
1760	Bifocal Glasses	Benjamin Franklin	A single set of glasses which corrects for both near and long sighted vision
1764	Spinning Jenny	James Hargreaves	Reduced amount of work it took to make yarn
1765	Steam Engine	James Watt	Early engine which revolutionized transportation
1785	Power Loom	Edmond Cartwright	Mechanically operated loom (made cloth)
1794	Cotton Gin	Eli Whitney	Separated cotton seeds from fibers quickly
1800	Battery	Count Allesandro Volta	First generator of continuous electrical current

Social and Political Developments

Since the end of World War II, the world might be described as increasingly interdependent. After a period of considering some nations "third world" countries, efforts to "globalize" have affected the West as well.

Interdependence brought about by scientific, technological, and industrial progress has carried the message of economic development to every nation on earth. Every government strives to improve the standard of living of its citizens in a variety of ways. Improved health, sanitation, and nutrition; broader educational training and employment opportunities; better housing, clothing, and other basic necessities; affordable entertainment; reasonably priced consumer goods; and more leisure time—all of these are elements of economic development.

Accomplishing these things requires the investment of money and human effort, both of which may be strained by the great need. Political leaders must make decisions and set policies, although there may be differing opinions about how their nation can best develop economically. Within a nation, even close political partners can disagree about how to achieve economic development.

The developing nations need to increase their agricultural production to keep up with the population increases in their nations. The efforts of scientists and government leaders to find ways to do this have produced a Green Revolution, that is, an increase in the amount of agricultural production from land already under cultivation and expansion of farming onto previously nonproductive land.

The basis of these improvements has been the development by agronomists (agricultural scientists) of high-yielding plant varieties. These are seeds that can produce greater quantities of crops (especially food grains such as rice and wheat) from an area of land than traditional seeds can produce. However, the new grains are not always as hardy as the older ones, and they need chemical fertilizers, more water, and pesticides to protect them from diseases and insects. Different farming techniques are also necessary to use them effectively.

The Green Revolution needs government support to be carried out. Governments must provide education and information as well as loans to enable farmers to buy the new seeds and the necessary pesticides and fertilizers. They must also build irrigation and transportation systems and provide price supports to guarantee that farmers can sell their products at a profit. In addition, governments must carry out land reform, distributing land in a more equal fashion. Finally, a technology for the Green Revolution (appropriate farm machines and techniques) that is useful in small areas at low cost must be developed and made available.

The Enlightenment was an intellectual movement characterized by a belief in reason and rationality. It emphasized science and knowledge and refused the ideas of superstition. A large portion of Enlightenment thinkers originated in France, though the movement was spread throughout Europe and even into the Americas. One of the primary figures of the Enlightenment was John Locke. Locke theorized extensively about the role of governments, arguing that men were rational but that government was a necessary compromise of society. He believed in three natural rights that should be afforded to all men regardless of circumstance: life, liberty and property.

Another important figure of the Enlightenment was Denis Diderot, whose 27 volume *Encyclopedie* is an excellent example of the Enlightenment ideal of the pursuit of knowledge. Baron de Montesquieu was also an important philosopher who is most famous for the concept of separation of powers, which is now used in governments throughout the world.

Cesare Beccaria was an Italian mind of the Enlightenment who was primarily concerned with the justice system. His book *On Crimes and Punishments* criticized the inefficiency of the current justice systems and condemned torture and the death penalty. The method of inductive reasoning was also a product of the Enlightenment, proposed by Sir Francis Bacon. Voltaire was also an Enlightenment philosopher, whose many writings advocated the freedoms of religion and speech among other things.

Jean-Jacques Rousseau championed the idea of a social contract which exists between citizens and governments, under which governments are obligated to protect the rights of the people. Other important Enlightenment thinkers include Thomas Hobbes, Adam Smith, Mozart, Immanuel Kant and Rene Descartes. In addition, many of the founding fathers of the United States are considered to have been influenced by the principles of the Enlightenment, such as Thomas Jefferson, Thomas Paine and Benjamin Franklin.

A number of eighteenth century rulers are often referred to as enlightened despots. Most notable of these enlightened despots are Catherine the Great of Russia, Joseph II of Austria and Frederick the Great of Prussia. The term refers to an attitude which these rulers had in which they were more concerned with improving the lives of their citizens than they were in maintaining or exercising power. For example, Frederick the Great referred to himself as the "first servant of the state," and worked to institute freedom of the press and religious tolerance among other things. Catherine the Great also reduced censorship and promoted education. In Austria, Joseph II reformed the government so that greater religious tolerance was practiced, and financial and judicial agencies were more responsible to the monarchy. The actions of these rulers were greatly influenced by the humanistic and other principles of the Enlightenment period.

🎓 *Sample Test Questions*

1) The noble revolts known as the Fronde resulted in

   A) The assassination of Cardinal Mazarin in 1661
   B) Renewed power for the Parliament of Paris
   C) A unified noble army securing and increasing its own power
   D) French citizens turning to the monarchy for stability
   E) The establishment of Catholicism as France's only legal religion

The correct answer is D:) French citizens turning to the monarchy for stability. The two Fronde revolts of 1648–1649 and 1651–1652 opposed the regency government of the Italian Cardinal Mazarin who attempted to centralize monarchical rule while governing for the underage Louis XIV.

2) The economic policies of Jean-Baptiste Colbert, Louis XIV's controller general of finances,

   A) Were noted for their innovation and originality
   B) Used new accounting practices to lessen the tax burden on the peasants
   C) Were based on mercantilism and stressed state benefits from government regulation of the economy
   D) Gave Louis the large treasury surplus he needed to make war
   E) Led to a policy of peace instead of war because of the latter's great economic costs

The correct answer is C:) Were based on mercantilism and stressed state benefits from government regulation of the economy. Louis XIV's controller general of finance, Jean-Baptiste Colbert, was a mercantilist. He favored a heavily regulated economy designed to increase the gold reserves in state coffers.

3) The War of the Spanish Succession was effectively concluded with the Peace of Utrecht in 1713, which

    A) Gave the French king control of Spanish territories
    B) Gave France control over the Spanish Netherlands, Naples, and Milan
    C) Drove the Bourbons from Spain
    D) Destroyed the European balance of power
    E) Greatly benefited England, a strong naval power

The correct answer is E:) Greatly benefited England, a strong naval power. The Treaty of Utrecht, which ended the War of the Spanish Succession, allowed the Bourbons to rule Spain but stated that the two Bourbon kingdoms of Spain and France would never be united.

4) During the reign of Philip IV, Spain

    A) Suffered under the misrule of the Duke of Lerma
    B) Won back its European possessions in the Thirty Years' War
    C) Received a respite from the civil wars and internal revolts common under Philip's predecessors
    D) Failed to make any real progress, despite reforms under the count of Olivares
    E) Lost most of its empire in the New World to England

The correct answer is D:) Failed to make any real progress, despite reforms under the count of Olivares. Spain's power declined significantly after the death of Philip II in 1598.

5) The Austrian Empire in the seventeenth century

    A) Was unified by linguistic and ethnic ties
    B) Was defeated at Vienna by a Turkish army in 1687
    C) Was a highly centralized, absolutist state under Leopold I
    D) Lost a German empire, but gained one in Eastern Europe
    E) Was successful in spreading Roman Catholicism throughout Eastern Europe, including Russia

The correct answer is D:) Lost a German empire, but gained one in Eastern Europe. Following the Thirty Years' War (1618–1648), the Austrian Habsburgs were forced to abandon their ambition to establish a strong empire in Germany.

6) The political institution known as the Sejm made seventeenth-century Poland

   A) An absolutist, monarchical state dominated by King Sigismund III
   B) A powerful militaristic machine threatening its neighbors
   C) A land without powerful nobles
   D) A constitutional monarchy, similar to that of England
   E) An impotent, decentralized state

The correct answer is E:) An impotent, decentralized state. Poland's Sejm was Poland's diet or parliament, a two-house legislature dominated by the landed aristocracy.

7) The MOST significant Romanov ruler of the eighteenth century was

   A) Ivan the Terrible
   B) Nicholas III
   C) Olaf the Great
   D) Peter the Great
   E) Michael

The correct answer is D:) Peter the Great. The most significant Romanov tsar of eighteenth–century Russia was Peter the Great (r. 1689–1725). Peter decided to westernize Russia and toured Western nations looking for ideas.

8) The "Glorious Revolution" in 1688 in England was significant for

   A) Restoring Charles II and the Stuart dynasty to power
   B) Bloodlessly deposing James II in favor of William of Orange
   C) Returning England to a Catholic commonwealth
   D) Parliament's establishment of a new monarch through a series of bloody wars
   E) The separation of England from Scotland

The correct answer is B:) Bloodlessly deposing James II in favor of William of Orange. James II sparked the Glorious Revolution when he suspended laws in an effort to restore Catholicism in England. In 1688, William of Orange invaded England with broad support from England's elite and drove James into exile.

9) Thomas Hobbes

    A) Believed that a state of nature without government or social institutions best ensured human happiness
    B) Stated that mankind was animalistic and needed a strong government to maintain social order
    C) Was a firm believer in representative democracy
    D) Supported theocratic rule under the guidance of the Vatican
    E) Declared that the institution of divine right meant that monarchy was the best form of government

The correct answer is B:) Stated that mankind was animalistic and needed a strong government to maintain social order. In 1651, Thomas Hobbes published his Leviathan, which was based on observations made during the violent upheavals of the English Civil War of the prior decade. Hobbes believed that humans benefited greatly from the social cohesion provide by a strong state.

10) In her Instruction, Catherine the Great outlined enlightened legal reforms that

    A) Abolished serfdom throughout Russia
    B) Established equality before the law for all Russian citizens
    C) Instigated changes in the Russian government that sapped the power of the old nobility
    D) Accomplished little and were soon forgotten due to heavy opposition
    E) Ended capital punishment

The correct answer is D:) Accomplished little and were soon forgotten due to heavy opposition. Catherine the Great corresponded with several of the Enlightenment philosophes and decided to reform Russia. In her Instruction (1767), she criticized serfdom, the use of torture and capital punishment, and advocated the principle of equality. Her attempts at reform failed, and her Instruction was quickly forgotten.

11) Catherine the Great of Russia

    A) Followed a successful policy of expansion against the Turks
    B) Instigated enlightened reforms for the peasantry after the revolt of Emelyn Pugachev
    C) Alienated the nobility with her extensive enlightened reforms
    D) Successfully eliminated the power of the Duma
    E) Was driven out of European Russia by Prussia's Frederick the Great

The correct answer is A:) Followed a successful policy of expansion against the Turks. Catherine the Great, like Peter the Great, was an expansionist tsar.

12) With regard to politics, King Frederick the Great of Prussia believed that the fundamental rule of governments is to

   A) Respect new human rights
   B) Expand their territories
   C) Combat church fanaticism
   D) Raise taxes to meet all military needs of state spending
   E) Equalizing social and economic differences among its citizens

The correct answer is B:) Expand their territories. Frederick II the Great of Prussia was one of the most intellectual rulers of the eighteenth century and corresponded extensively with Voltaire.

13) Which of the following financial advantages did the British government enjoyed over French rulers of the eighteenth century?

   A) Britain could borrow large sums of money at low rates of interest.
   B) The British government had a lower total amount of debt.
   C) Britain had a strong policy against state borrowing of any kind.
   D) France had no real curbs on its borrowing.
   E) Britain lacked costly colonial obligations and responsibilities.

The correct answer is A:) Britain could borrow large sums of money at low rates of interest. The Bank of England was established in 1694, allowing the British government to borrow large sums of money at low interest rates.

14) Improvements in eighteenth-century European agricultural methods and practices occurred primarily in

   A) France
   B) The Netherlands
   C) Britain
   D) Russia
   E) Poland

The correct answer is C:) Britain. In the eighteenth century, England led the Agricultural Revolution.

15) All of these authorities were relied on by medieval scholars EXCEPT

   A) Aristotle
   B) Galen
   C) Ptolemy
   D) Curie
   E) Archimedes

The correct answer is D:) Curie. Aristotle was a Greek philosopher of the fourth century BCE, Galen was a Greek physician of the second century CE, Claudius Ptolemy was an astronomer of the second century CE, and Archimedes was a scientist and mathematician from the third century BCE. All would have been influential in the Middle Ages. However, Marie Curie could not have been, inasmuch as she was worked in the twentieth century.

16) Galileo's observations resulted in the dramatic finding that the

   A) Orbits of planets were elliptical rather than circular
   B) Planets were made of materials similar to those found on Earth
   C) The solar system was much larger than previously thought
   D) The stars were smaller than previously thought
   E) Jupiter had more rings than Saturn

The correct answer is B:) Planets were made of materials similar to those found on Earth. Galileo used his telescope to discover that other bodies of the universe were composed of substances similar to those making up the earth.

17) Which of the following Greco-Roman doctors had the GREATEST influence on medieval medical thought?

   A) Hippocrates
   B) Rhazes
   C) Galen
   D) Aristotle
   E) Paracelsus

The correct answer is C:) Galen. Late medieval medical theory was dominated by the ideas of second-century CE Greek physician, Galen. His influence was profound in anatomy, physiology, disease theories, and in medical practices.

18) William Harvey's On the Motion of the Heart and Blood refuted the idea that the

    A) Immune system was governed by the pancreas
    B) Liver was the beginning point of circulation of blood
    C) Lymph system functioned independently
    D) Traditional herbal healing methods were effective blood cleansers
    E) Primary transmission of disease was through bad blood

The correct answer is B:) Liver was the beginning point of circulation of blood. William Harvey's *On the Motion of the Heart and Blood*, published in 1628, refuted Galen's contention that the liver was the beginning point in the circulation of blood.

19) Descartes believed that the world could be understood using

    A) The same principles inherent in mathematical thinking
    B) Quiet contemplation of the Holy Scriptures
    C) Lessons learned from mystical experiences
    D) Insights gained from the interpretation of dreams
    E) An imagined tabula rasa

The correct answer is A:) The same principles inherent in mathematical thinking. In 1619, Descartes first proposed that the world could be understood using the same principles as those inherent in mathematics.

20) Why did Russia extricate itself from WWI?

    A) They had run out of resources and could not continue fighting.
    B) After losing ground in Stalingrad they believed that they would do better to end the war quickly.
    C) They were responding to a bribe offered by Germany to quit fighting.
    D) Political turmoil had arisen due to the Bolshevik Revolution.
    E) None of the above

The correct answer is D:) Political turmoil had arisen due to the Bolshevik Revolution. Due to these factors, Vladimir Lenin, a Bolshevik leader, wanted the country out of World War I at any cost.

21) Spinoza believed that a failure to understand God led

    A) To the false worship of nature
    B) People to use nature for their own self-interest
    C) Individuals to incorrectly judge the morality of others
    D) The faithful to sexual perversion
    E) To a separation of mind and body

The correct answer is B:) People to use nature for their own self-interest. Benedict de Spinoza was a pantheist who believed that God was the universe, not just the creator of the universe.

22) Which of the following statements is FALSE regarding the Treaty of Versailles?

    A) It had little effect on Germany as they were not even invited to the negotiations.
    B) The treaty required that Germany make large reparations payments.
    C) The treaty required that Germany limit the size of their military.
    D) The treaty required that Germany admit to guilt in WWI.
    E) All of the above statements are accurate.

The correct answer is A:) It had little effect on Germany as they were not even invited to the negotiations. The requirements of the treaty allowed Hitler to rise to power on a platform of the unfair treatment that Germany had received at the hands of the Allied powers.

23) Which of the following was a key figure of the Scientific Revolution who inspired the search for natural laws in numerous fields, including sociology and economics?

    A) Galileo
    B) Newton
    C) Descartes
    D) Pascal
    E) Copernicus

The correct answer is B:) Newton. Isaac Newton who created mechanistic and orderly explanations for a number of physical phenomena was a key figure of the Scientific Revolution.

24) The French philosophes

    A) Were literate intellectuals who hoped to change the world using reason and rationality
    B) Flourished in an atmosphere of government support
    C) Sought to prevent the expansion of the Enlightenment to other states
    D) Encouraged state censorship of ideas contrary to their own
    E) Were academic philosophers associated with the University of Paris and other French universities

The correct answer is A:) Were literate intellectuals who hoped to change the world using reason and rationality. Intellectuals in the Enlightenment were known by the French term philosophes, although not all were French or formal philosophers.

25) After which of the following did the Bolsheviks take power and create the first Soviet government headed by Lenin?

    A) When Lenin gave his April Theses
    B) February Revolution
    C) October Revolution
    D) WWII
    E) None of the above

The correct answer is C:) October Revolution. Through it the Bolsheviks took power of the major city of Petrograd. The Revolution resulted in the first Soviet government, headed by Lenin, and the revolution spread throughout the country.

26) Which of the following cities was the recognized capital of the Enlightenment?

    A) Geneva
    B) Berlin
    C) London
    D) Paris
    E) Rome

The correct answer is D:) Paris. Paris was the recognized capital of the Enlightenment.

27) European intellectual life of the eighteenth century was marked by the emergence of

    A) Anti-Semitism and greater persecution of minorities
    B) Secularization and a search to find the natural laws governing human life
    C) Sophism and the mockery of past traditions
    D) Monastic schools and medieval modes of religious training
    E) The separation of the institutions of church and state across all of Europe

The correct answer is B:) Secularization and a search to find the natural laws governing human life. The Scientific Revolution was a major turning point in Western history.

28) Diderot's contributions to Enlightenment efforts against religious fanaticism, intolerance, and prudery is BEST exemplified in his

    A) Brilliant play "Is Rome Burning?"
    B) Twenty-eight volume encyclopedia compiling articles from numerous philosophes
    C) Autobiography published in French
    D) Biography of Newton, "the greatest Europe has ever known"
    E) Confessions

The correct answer is B:) Twenty-eight volume encyclopedia compiling articles from numerous philosophes. Denis Diderot's major contribution to the Enlightenment was his twenty-eight volume Encyclopedia, or Classified Dictionary of the Sciences, Arts, and Trades.

29) Which country was NOT represented at the Paris Peace Conference?

    A) Britain
    B) France
    C) Austria
    D) Russia
    E) Germany

The correct answer is E:) Germany. Despite the fact that they received no representation, the Treaty of Versailles had enormous impact on the future of Germany.

30) Which ruler is famed for instituting a series of five year plans?

    A) Mao Zedong
    B) Lenin
    C) Catherine the Great
    D) Stalin
    E) Ceasare Beccaria

The correct answer is D:) Stalin. He instituted three main five year plans which resulted in rapid industrialization and subjugation of the people.

31) Deism was based on

    A) Newton's conception of a rational universe following scientific laws
    B) God answering prayers directed to him in song and poetry
    C) The divinity of Jesus as son of the prime mover of the rational universe
    D) The denial of the existence of any Supreme Being
    E) The pantheism of Spinoza and other enlightened philosophers

The correct answer is A:) Newton's conception of a rational universe following scientific laws. Deism was an outgrowth of Newton's world-machine.

32) In *The Social Contract*, Rousseau expressed his belief that

    A) Government was an evil that should be eliminated
    B) An individual's will is most important
    C) Freedom is achieved by being forced to follow the "general will," or what is best for all
    D) A child was a small adult with all the same abilities and obligations
    E) In nature, human life was "solitary, poor, nasty, brutish, and short"

The correct answer is C:) Freedom is achieved by being forced to follow the "general will," or what is best for all. In *The Social Contract*, Jean Jacques Rousseau argued that government was a necessary evil, created to preserve private property.

33) High culture in eighteenth-century Europe was influenced by the

    A) Enormous impact of the book publishing industry
    B) Decline of French as an international language
    C) Decline of magazine circulations with the rise of the novel
    D) Increased dependency of authors on wealthy patrons
    E) Its exclusive focus upon religious subject matter

The correct answer is A:) Enormous impact of the book publishing industry. Latin was the international language of eighteenth-century European elite scientists, philosophers, poets, dramatists and other intellectuals. However, the expansion of book publishing revolutionized European high culture, as the use of national languages produced an increase in the exchange of ideas between elites and the new reading public of the middle class.

34) The punishment of crime in the eighteenth century was often

    A) Public and very gruesome
    B) Carried out by mobs after the criminals were charged in court
    C) Less severe than the crime would merit
    D) The responsibility of the army
    E) Reduced to probation and fines due to the influence of the churches and philosophers

The correct answer is A:) Public and very gruesome. Punishments for crime in the eighteenth century were cruel and gruesome.

35) John Wesley

    A) Was responsible for the resurgence of Catholic piety
    B) Supported a rationalistic approach to Protestantism
    C) Spread the teachings of pietism through his Moravian Brethren
    D) Created and controlled his evangelical Methodist church using revivalist techniques
    E) Was a leading Deist

The correct answer is D:) Created and controlled his evangelical Methodist church using revivalist techniques. The established churches of the eighteenth century offered followers little spiritual reward.

36) Why did the US come to the aid of the Greek government during the Greek Civil War in the 1940's?

   A) To stop the country from falling to communism.
   B) To avoid a financial collapse that would have devastated Europe.
   C) To extend their reach into Mediterranean business.
   D) To show a dedicated interest in rebuilding Europe after WWII.
   E) None of the above

The correct answer is A:) To stop the country from falling to communism. When the Greek Civil War weakened the country and threatened to result in its conversion to communism, President Truman requested that Congress grant them financial and military aid through the Truman Doctrine.

37) Napoleon's Continental System was meant to harm which country?

   A) Russia
   B) Germany
   C) France
   D) Britain
   E) India

The correct answer is D:) Britain. By 1806 Napoleon had managed to conquer most of mainland Europe, and so he set his sights on Britain and began the Continental System.

38) The American colonists were able win their war for independence because of

   A) Generous military and financial aid from France
   B) The collapse of the English colonial system
   C) Apathy of the English military
   D) Flaws in the English mercantile system
   E) George III's recognition of colonial independence 1776

The correct answer is A:) Generous military and financial aid from France. Economic and military assistance provided by France and other European nations were a crucial factor in the American fight for independence.

39) The American Revolution had which of the following effects on Europeans?

    A) Showing that military force was the final diplomatic authority
    B) Ending colonial expansion around the world
    C) Establishing that the new United States was the most powerful nation
    D) Demonstrating that the ideas of the Enlightenment could be realized politically
    E) Revealing that mighty England could be defeated

The correct answer is D:) Demonstrating that the ideas of the Enlightenment could be realized politically. The American Revolution showed Europeans that the ideas of the Enlightenment could be implemented successfully to form a new society.

40) Which of the following was the MOST immediate cause of the French Revolution?

    A) The government failed to resolve its debt and other economic problems.
    B) Reforms were blocked by the French Parliament.
    C) The philosophes called for radical reforms.
    D) Louis XVI's rejected the cahiers de doléances.
    E) Peasant rioted in the countryside.

The correct answer is A:) The government failed to resolve its debt and other economic problems. The French economy grew well during the second half of the eighteenth century, despite bad harvests in 1787 and 1788 that led to food shortages.

41) The economic restructuring implemented by Gorbachev was called

    A) Communism
    B) Marxism
    C) Capitalism
    D) Continental System
    E) Perestroika

The correct answer is E:) Perestroika

42) Compared to the American Revolution, the French Revolution was

   A) More violent
   B) More radical
   C) More influential in Europe as a model of rebellion
   D) More influential to most of the world outside Europe as a model of revolution
   E) All of the above

The correct answer is E:) All of the above. Although the American Revolution had considerable influence in Europe and in France, the French Revolution was more violent (e.g. the execution of Louis XVI and the Terror of 1793–1794), more radical (e.g. full male democracy, the worship of pure reason, the revolutionary calendar), and more influential both in Europe and the rest of the world as a model of revolution (e.g. Russian Revolution of 1917 and the Chinese Communist Revolution of 1946–1949).

43) Of the following, who was responsible for killing more of their own people?

   A) Lenin
   B) Mao Zedong
   C) Hitler
   D) Stalin
   E) Unknown

The correct answer is B:) Mao Zedong. Estimates of the number killed under Mao's rule are 40 million people (with some estimates ranging to nearly twice that number) – nearly twice that of Stalin.

44) In 1789, the Estates-General

   A) Was an advisory body that was often consulted by King Louis XVI
   B) Unanimously agreed that only radical change could solve France's problems
   C) Was dominated by the First Estate composed mostly of urban lawyers
   D) Was deeply divided over the issue of whether to vote by Estates or by head
   E) Was trying to seize power from the National Assembly

The correct answer is D:) Was deeply divided over the issue of whether to vote by Estates or by head. When the Estates-General assembled at Versailles in May 1789, members immediately disagreed over what voting procedure to follow.

45) The book *J'accuse* was instrumental in spreading information about which scandal?

    A) Dreyfus affair
    B) Widespread bribery
    C) Wilson case
    D) Boulanger affair
    E) None of the above

The correct answer is A:) Dreyfus affair. The accusatory *J'accuse* was useful in spreading outrage over the cover up and other incidences of corruption in the French government.

46) Just prior to the Revolution in France, the number of poor people in France

    A) Declined
    B) Increased greatly
    C) Increased slightly
    D) Remained the same
    E) Declined slightly

The correct answer is B:) Increased greatly. The number of poor in France in the late eighteenth century is estimated at being about one third of the total population.

47) What position did the United States take in the Korean War?

    A) Supported South Korea under the Truman Doctrine
    B) Supported North Korea under the Truman Doctrine
    C) Supported South Korea due to the Brezhnev Doctrine
    D) Supported North Korea due to the Brezhnev Doctrine
    E) Neither, they took a neutral stand under the Communist Manifesto

The correct answer is A:) Supported South Korea under the Truman Doctrine. Fear of South Korea falling to communism spurred the United States' interest in the war in Korea.

48) Which of the following slogans from the French Revolution neatly evoked the ideals of the rebellion?

    A) "Down with the aristocracy!"
    B) "Liberty, Equality, Fraternity!"
    C) "Death to the king and queen!"
    D) "Kill all priests and burn all churches!"
    E) "Vive l'Empereur!"

The correct answer is B:) "Liberty, Equality, Fraternity!" The upheavals of the French Revolution led to new liberal and national political ideals most famously expressed in the slogan, "Liberty, Equality, Fraternity!"

49) The Bastille was

    A) The king's castle
    B) An arsenal and prison
    C) The place where most state executions took place
    D) A monastery
    E) A royal palace

The correct answer is B:) An arsenal and prison. The Bastille was an old medieval fortress in Paris.

50) What is considered to be the first armed conflict of the Cold War?

    A) Battle of Versailles
    B) Korean War
    C) Greek Civil War
    D) Vietnam War
    E) Battle of Stalingrad

The correct answer is B:) Korean War. With both portions of Korea being supported by much stronger powers, the war was really a product of the Cold War.

51) The National Assembly's approach towards the Catholic Church was to

    A) Leave the institution alone
    B) Increase its power dramatically in France
    C) Pass legislation to secularize the church offices and clergy
    D) Ban Catholicism from France
    E) Force the Church to ordain women as priests

The correct answer is C:) Pass legislation to secularize the church offices and clergy. The Catholic Church was a symbol of the Old Regime and therefore very unpopular among many of the revolutionaries.

52) The Brezhnev Doctrine was

    A) A direct response by USSR leader Leonid Brezhnev to the Truman Doctrine.
    B) A statement issued by USSR leader Leonid Brezhnev and stated that once a country had become communist, it would stay that way forever.
    C) An explanation of the socialist concepts set forth by Brezhnev shortly before WWI.
    D) A decree by German leaders that cooperation with Russia would not be granted.
    E) None of the above

The correct answer is B:) A statement issued by USSR leader Leonid Brezhnev and stated that once a country had become communist, it would stay that way forever.

53) During the 1790s, the army of the French Republic

    A) Received little backing from the home front
    B) Was small but effective in battle
    C) Continued to be commanded by members of the Bourbon family
    D) Was totally defeated by foreign aristocratic forces
    E) Fueled modern nationalism and was raised through total mobilization of the population

The correct answer is E:) Fueled modern nationalism and was raised through total mobilization of the population. Although revolutionary ideals were supposed to give France victory against its foreign royalist enemies, by 1793 French armies suffered defeats and a foreign coalition was poised to invade France.

54) The French Revolution was led by members of the

    A) First Estate
    B) Lower Second Estate
    C) Lower Third Estate
    D) Proletariat
    E) Bourgeoisie

The correct answer is E:) Bourgeoisie. The bourgeoisie were the main leaders of the French Revolution who were disgusted by the attitudes of the aristocracy and their treatment of the Third Estate.

55) Which of the following statements best describes the Dreyfus affair?

    A) It was discovered that Captain Dreyfus had been involved in altering communications with French allies in an effort to prolong the war.
    B) German officer Alfred Dreyfus was discovered to have been falsely accused of murder, but was sentenced to death anyway.
    C) French Captain Dreyfus was falsely accused of giving information to the Germans on a basis of forged evidence and wrongful trial proceedings.
    D) Captain Dreyfus was discovered to have Soviet sympathies and was relieved of his post during World War II.
    E) None of the above

The correct answer is C:) French Captain Dreyfus was falsely accused of giving information to the Germans on a basis of forged evidence and wrongful trial proceedings.

56) Napoleon's rapid rise to power was based on his

    A) Series of stunning defeats over the enemies of France
    B) Social programs that appealed to the masses
    C) Promises to make France great again
    D) Supporters within an inner clique of revolutionaries dedicated to the general
    E) Personal charisma and his family connections to the Bourbons

The correct answer is A:) Series of stunning defeats over the enemies of France. Napoleon was an outsider born on the island of Corsica and would never have achieved high rank or status in France under the royalist regime.

57) The Truman Doctrine instituted a policy of

    A) Direct Intervention
    B) Containment
    C) Enlightened Absolutism
    D) Abolitionism
    E) None of the above

The correct answer is B:) Containment. In other words, the United States committed to stop the spread of communism, or contain it.

58) Which of the following was NOT a factor that contributed to Napoleon's defeat?

    A) The failure of the Continental System
    B) The defeat of the French navy at the Battle of Trafalgar
    C) The unmanageable rebellions provoked by his brutal rule over conquered countries
    D) The spread of nationalism in the conquered countries
    E) The invasion of Russia

The correct answer is C:) The unmanageable rebellions provoked by his brutal rule over conquered countries. Although Napoleon was still at war with Britain and needed to maintain order in conquered countries, his rule reflected the ideals of the Revolution and the Enlightenment.

59) Klemens von Metternich

    A) Continued to incorporate revolutionary values into his government following Napoleon's defeat
    B) Believed that a free press was necessary to maintain the status quo in Europe
    C) Was a political reactionary, but believed that a republic was the best way to ensure order
    D) Was anti-religious and supported atheistic causes in Eastern Europe and Russia
    E) Believed European monarchs shared a common interest in promoting stability

The correct answer is E:) Believed European monarchs shared a common interest in promoting stability. Prince Klemens von Metternich, the Austrian foreign minister, was the key figure at the Congress of Vienna that ended the Napoleonic wars.

60) France lost the provinces of Alsace and Lorraine to Germany as a result of which war?

    A) WWI
    B) WWII
    C) Korean War
    D) Vietnamese War
    E) Franco-Prussian War

The correct answer is E:) Franco-Prussian War. Through war with Germany, Otto von Bismarck was able to unify the states (the largest of which was his own Prussia). The treaty additionally transferred the provinces Alsace and Lorraine to Germany, and required that France pay five million francs.

61) The Industrial Revolution in Britain was largely inspired by

    A) An urgent need to reduce eighteenth-century poverty
    B) The failure of the cottage industry
    C) Entrepreneurs who sought and accepted the new manufacturing methods of inventions
    D) The Dutch and French industrialization
    E) The availability of substantial amounts of English-grown cotton

The correct answer is C:) Entrepreneurs who sought and accepted the new manufacturing methods of inventions. The Industrial Revolution in Britain was inspired by entrepreneurs who sought out and applied new manufacturing methods and technologies.

62) The invention of the steam engine in Britain was initially triggered by

    A) The textile industry's demand for new sources of power
    B) Problems in the mining industry
    C) The railroad industry's call for a more efficient source of power
    D) The need for a more efficient mode of power for English ships
    E) The need to replace sailing ships with steam power

The correct answer is B:) Problems in the mining industry. The problem of water seepage deep in British coal mines spurred on the invention of the steam engine.

63) The first policy which the Truman Doctrine was used in support of was

A) Korean War
B) Vietnamese War
C) WWII
D) Greek Civil War
E) None of the above

The correct answer is D:) Greek Civil War. When the Greek Civil War weakened the country and threatened to result in its conversion to communism, President Truman requested that Congress grant them financial and military aid.

64) The success of the steam engine in the Industrial Revolution made Britain dependent upon

A) Timber
B) Coal
C) Water power
D) Electricity
E) Railroads

The correct answer is B:) Coal. Britain was fortunate to have considerable iron and coal deposits.

65) Which of the following BEST describes Gorbachev's economic plan?

A) Increased government regulation to force the economy into revitalization.
B) Decreased government regulation to make the people realize how much they needed the government to control things.
C) Increased government control to put the economy back onto a more successful path.
D) Decreased government control to encourage people to have a more hopeful attitude and revitalize the economy.
E) None of the above

The correct answer is D:) Decreased government control to encourage people to have a more hopeful attitude and revitalize the economy. Gorbachev hoped to revitalize the economy by changing the attitudes about working. He instituted better working conditions and increased leisure time.

66) The rise of the industrial factory system deeply changed the quality of life and social status of workers who

    A) Were traditionally paid in kind
    B) Lost ownership of the means of production, becoming simple wage earners
    C) Were less vulnerable to more rapid cycles of economic boom and bust
    D) Got both good wages and many fringe benefits unknown before
    E) Saw entire family units working together in factories

The correct answer is B:) Lost ownership of the means of production, becoming simple wage earners. The replacement of cottage industries by industrial factories radically changed workers' lives.

67) The Paris Peace Conference was where negotiations took place at the end of which war?

    A) French Revolution
    B) WWI
    C) Franco-Prussian War
    D) WWII
    E) Korean War

The correct answer is B:) WWI. At the end of World War I it was agreed that there would be a peace conference held in Paris to determine the fate of the Central Powers. This is now referred to as the Paris Peace Conference.

68) Industrialization began on the continent first in

    A) Spain and Italy
    B) Austria and Poland
    C) Russia and Sweden
    D) Norway and Denmark
    E) Belgium and Germany

The correct answer is E:) Belgium and Germany. Industrialization began on the continent first in Belgium and Germany, along with France.

69) Which scientist first proposed the Heliocentric model of the solar system?

    A) Ptolemy
    B) Galileo
    C) Copernicus
    D) Kepler
    E) Newton

The correct answer is C:) Copernicus. Generally considered to be the first monumental event of the scientific revolution is the proposal of the Heliocentric model (sun centered model) of the solar system by Nicolas Copernicus.

70) Which scientist is famed for developing three Laws of Motion?

    A) Ptolemy
    B) Galileo
    C) Copernicus
    D) Kepler
    E) Newton

The correct answer is E:) Newton. Sir Isaac Newton's three laws are namely, the principle of inertia, the relationship between force and acceleration, and the idea of equal and opposite reactions.

71) The Industrial Revolution in continental Europe

    A) Was a generation behind Britain in cotton manufacture
    B) Neglected coal and iron technology in favor of the progress in the textile industry
    C) Benefited from the discovery of vast coal deposits in Germany in the 1820's
    D) Would remain far behind the British until the twentieth century
    E) Quickly surpassed Britain's production of cotton cloth

The correct answer is A:) Was a generation behind Britain in cotton manufacture. Even France, the continental leader in cotton production, lagged far behind Great Britain.

72) Which treaty was negotiated at the end of WWI?

    A) Brest-Litovsk Treaty
    B) Treaty of Frankfurt
    C) Treaty of Paris
    D) Treaty of Versailles
    E) None of the above

The correct answer is D:) Treaty of Versailles. The Treaty of Versailles was negotiated at the Paris Peace Conference.

73) The European population explosion of the nineteenth century was

    A) The result of increased birthrates across Europe
    B) Largely attributable to the disappearance of famine from much of Europe
    C) Caused by a lack of emigration
    D) Remarkable because of the preponderance of major epidemic diseases
    E) Limited to Catholic countries

The correct answer is B:) Largely attributable to the disappearance of famine from much of Europe. The nineteenth-century increase in European population was due primarily to improved food supplies that virtually eliminated famine. Medical advances and improved sanitation also reduced disease deaths, and there were fewer major wars than in previous centuries. Birthrates had actually begun to decline after 1790.

74) Industrialization produced many demographic changes and caused the

    A) Landed aristocracy to move from cities to escape the ill effects of factory development
    B) New middle class to move to the suburbs of cities to escape the urban poor
    C) Newly affluent laboring class to live in diverse locations
    D) Rich and poor to live together more often in new suburban housing developments
    E) Rich to build large mansions and palaces close to the urban seats of government

The correct answer is B:) New middle class to move to the suburbs of cities to escape the urban poor. An urban explosion took place in the nineteenth century, largely as a consequence of the Industrial Revolution.

75) Which of the following best describes Pascal's Wager?

    A) A bet made by Pascal that WWII would not end within three years.
    B) A belief that it is better to bet than God does exist than live as though he doesn't.
    C) The argument that most of the major governments of Europe would consolidate by 1850.
    D) A belief that most people would not rebel against their leaders when given the chance.
    E) None of the above

The correct answer is B:) A belief that it is better to bet than God does exist than live as though he doesn't.

76) The Luddites

    A) Received little support in their areas of activity
    B) Destroyed industrial machines that threatened their livelihood
    C) Were composed of the lowest unskilled workers in Great Britain
    D) Was the first movement of working-class consciousness of the Continent
    E) Were a phenomenon of continental industrialization

The correct answer is B:) Destroyed industrial machines that threatened their livelihood. The Luddites, led by a mythical "King Ludd" or "Ned Ludd," were skilled English craftsmen, mostly from the cotton cloth trade.

77) The Greek independence rebellion was successful largely because of

    A) A well-trained guerrilla army
    B) The Turks' lack of fortitude
    C) European intervention
    D) Superior Greek military tactics
    E) The superior Greeks defense of the acropolis

The correct answer is C:) European intervention. European intervention by France, Britain, and Russia helped Greeks to regain their freedom from the Ottomans in 1829.

78) Which of the following statements about Tsar Alexander I of Russia is NOT correct?

    A) He became more reactionary following the defeat of Napoleon.
    B) He promulgated a new constitution, freeing the serfs.
    C) He reformed the Russian education system.
    D) He adopted a program of arbitrary censorship to strengthen autocratic rule.
    E) He died without an heir in 1825, leading to a dispute over who should become the next tsar.

The correct answer is B:) He promulgated a new constitution, freeing the serfs. Alexander I (1800–1825) was raised to believe in Enlightenment ideals and began his reign as a reformer, relaxing censorship and improving the educational system.

79) What were the three natural rights proposed by John Locke?

    A) Life, liberty and the pursuit of happiness
    B) Safety, property and wealth
    C) Life, liberty and property
    D) Safety, means, and liberty
    E) Capitalism, safety and the pursuit of happiness

The correct answer is C:) Life, liberty and property. Locke also argued that men were rational, but that government was a necessary compromise of society.

80) Which of the following was a post-WWII plan to help rebuild Europe?

    A) Pascal's Wager
    B) Brezhnev Doctrine
    C) Paris Convention
    D) Marshall Plan
    E) Continental System

The correct answer is D:) Marshall Plan. The Marshall Plan was official called the European Recovery Plan and resulted in 13 billion dollars of aid being distributed to various European countries.

81) Which of the following best describes the Continental System?

   A) A blockade by European countries against trade with Britain.
   B) A blockade by Britain against trade with all other European countries.
   C) An attempt by Napoleon to unite the European continent into a single nation.
   D) A plan to erode the economic stability of Napoleon by forcing him to trade only with continental European countries.
   E) None of the above

The correct answer is A:) A blockade by European countries against trade with Britain. Through the Continental System Napoleon hoped to force Britain into depression, weakening their naval strength.

82) *Encyclopedie* was the work of

   A) Sir Isaac Newton
   B) Denis Diderot
   C) Jean-Jacques Rousseau
   D) Voltaire
   E) John Locke

The correct answer is B:) Denis Diderot. Diderot believed that all people had the right to educate themselves further. The first volume was published in 1751 and was followed over the years with 27 additional volumes.

83) Nineteenth-century liberalism was MOST warmly embraced by

   A) Factory workers
   B) The industrial middle class
   C) Radical aristocrats
   D) Wrmy officers
   E) Large landowners

The correct answer is B:) The industrial middle class. The industrial middle class warmly embraced the ideals of nineteenth-century liberalism.

84) Which of the following concepts did deists NOT reject?

A) Miracles
B) Superstitions
C) The existence of God
D) Bible
E) Prophecies

The correct answer is C:) The existence of God. Deism is a religious belief which affirms the existence of God, but does not believe him to intervene in daily life.

85) Which of the following individuals was NOT Deist?

A) Benjamin Franklin
B) Thomas Jefferson
C) John Lock
D) Sir Isaac Newton
E) Blase Pascal

The correct answer is E:) Blasé Pascal. Pascal was a deeply religious Christian, famous for Pascal's Wager.

86) The 1832, British Reform Bill primarily benefited the

A) Landed aristocracy
B) Upper-middle class
C) Working class
D) Clergy
E) Formally educated

The correct answer is B:) Upper-middle class. The upper middle class benefited the most from the Reform Bill of 1832.

87) Which of the following is NOT an invention of Blaise Pascal?

A) Syringe
B) Laws of probability
C) First mechanical calculator
D) All of the above are inventions of Blaise Pascal
E) None of the above

The correct answer is E:) None of the above. All of the inventions were creations of Pascal.

88) In 1848, the Frankfurt Assembly

A) Unanimously adopted a Grossdeutsch solution for the Germanies
B) Succeeded in making Prussia's Frederick William IV president of a united Germany
C) Failed in its attempt to create a united Germany
D) Gained the support of Austria
E) Successfully organized a military uprising that unified all of Germany under Prussian leadership

The correct answer is C:) Failed in its attempt to create a united Germany. The German Confederation's Frankfurt Assembly was dominated by educated middle-class delegates who were professors, lawyers, journalists, and bureaucrats.

89) The creation of professional police forces and prison improvements were geared toward

A) The creation of more disciplined and law-abiding societies
B) Lessening public outcry over poor living conditions for convicts
C) Protecting the poor from exploitation by businessmen and the rich
D) Adding an element of fear to society for psychological manipulation of mass populations
E) The rehabilitation and reintegration into society of the most violent criminals

The correct answer is A:) The creation of more disciplined and law-abiding societies. Prison reform and professional police forces of the nineteenth century were geared toward the creation of a more disciplined society.

90) The motivation behind the writing of Encyclopedie was

A) To preserve a record of everything that was known.
B) The author was paid a large sum by the Catholic church.
C) As a practice publication for the first printing press.
D) To describe the overarching principles of the Enlightenment.
E) None of the above

The correct answer is A:) To preserve a record of everything that was known. Diderot looked critically upon the Catholic Church, noting their historical tendency to destroy books and free thinkers. Encyclopedie was meant to combat this policy by containing a record of everything that was known, and thereby preserve the information.

91) The MOST important form of literary expression for the Romantics was

    A) The educational treatise
    B) Poetry
    C) The novel
    D) The play
    E) The historical biography

The correct answer is B:) Poetry. Sentiment and individualism formed the keystone of the Romantic movement, and Romantics considered poetry to be the most important form of literary expression.

92) The treaty by which Russia removed itself from WWI was the

    A) Treaty of Versailles
    B) Treaty of Stalingrad
    C) Brest-Litovsk Treaty
    D) Peace of Paris
    E) Peace of Westphalia

The correct answer is C:) Brest-Litovsk Treaty. As a result of the treaty, war was ended between Russia and the Central Powers. Russia was forced to surrender a significant amount of land, constituting nearly a quarter of their population and industry.

93) In economic matters, Napoleon III

    A) Had a laissez-faire attitude
    B) Gave to France a larger empire than even that of Britain
    C) Strove to diminish the power of great industrialists
    D) Established monopolies for foreign firms with expertise lacking in French firms
    E) Used government resources to stimulate the national economy and industrial growth

The correct answer is E:) Used government resources to stimulate the national economy and industrial growth. Napoleon III, like his uncle, Napoleon Bonaparte, was an authoritarian ruler.

94) Although it was an evolutionary process, the transformation of society to a consumer orientation can be traced back to the

    A) French Revolution
    B) Scientific Revolution
    C) American Revolution
    D) Invention of the printing press
    E) Industrial Revolution

The correct answer is E:) Industrial Revolution. After the Industrial Revolution, goods became available at increasingly low prices and in greater amounts.

95) The Red Shirts' leader whose military command helped unify Italy was

    A) Prince Napoleon
    B) Giuseppe Garibaldi
    C) Victor Emmanuel II
    D) Camillo di Cavour
    E) Charles Albert

The correct answer is B:) Giuseppe Garibaldi. In 1860, Giuseppe Garibaldi invaded Sicily with an army of a thousand Red Shirt volunteers.

96) Who was the first leader of the Bolshevik party?

    A) Stalin
    B) Mao Zedong
    C) Tsar Nicholas II
    D) Lenin
    E) None of the above

The correct answer is D:) Lenin. At the Second Congress of the Russian Social Democratic Labor Party two factions emerged: Bolshevik and Menshevik. The Bolsheviks were led by Lenin.

97) As prime minister of Prussia, Otto von Bismarck

A) Instituted important liberal land reforms
B) Largely bypassed parliament to pursue his goal to modernize the military
C) Was totally dependent on the Prussian military
D) Was extremely unpopular among ordinary Germans
E) Became the first German emperor in 1871 after the Franco-Prussian War

The correct answer is B:) Largely bypassed parliament to pursue his goal to modernize the military. Prussia's King William I wished to expand and modernize Prussia's military.

98) The Ausgleich, or Compromise, of 1867

A) Created a loose federation of ethnic states within the Austrian Empire
B) Freed the serfs and eliminated compulsory labor in the Austrian Empire
C) Made Austria part of the North German Confederation
D) Created the dual monarchy of Austria-Hungary
E) Destroyed the unity that had been achieved between Austria and Hungary in the 1848 revolutions

The correct answer is D:) Created the dual monarchy of Austria-Hungary. In the nineteenth century, ethnic nationalism was endemic in the German-run Austrian Empire, particularly in Hungary.

99) Which of the following was a motivation behind the Marshall Plan?

A) Combating communism
B) Colonization of Africa
C) Rebuilding Europe after WWII
D) Military victory in the Cold War
E) Both A and C

The correct answer is E:) Both A and C. The Marshall was created as a method of rebuilding the decimated European countries after WWII in an attempt to keep them from falling to communism.

100) Karl Marx embraced the German philosopher Hegel's idea of the dialectic, positing that

A) All change in history is the result of clashes between directly antagonistic elements
B) No real changes in society can occur before industrialization
C) Dictatorship is the central political force in all history
D) Political dialogs are the highest form of intellectual thought
E) Reality is spiritual and transcendent

The correct answer is A:) All change in history is the result of clashes between directly antagonistic elements. Karl Marx adopted Hegel's conception of the dialectic and applied it to the study of economic and social history.

101) The bourgeoisie were members of which of France's social classes?

A) First Estate
B) Second Estate
C) Third Estate
D) Fourth Estate
E) Capitalist class

The correct answer is C:) Third Estate. The First Estate was the clergy, the Second Estate was the aristocracy, or ruling class, and the Third Estate comprised everyone else – the wealthier end of which would have been the bourgeoisie.

102) Which of the following statements BEST applies to Charles Darwin and his evolutionary theory?

A) His ideas were readily accepted by religious fundamentalists and cultural conservatives.
B) His works were truly revolutionary and he was the first person to propose a theory of evolution.
C) He documented how natural selection governed the adaptation of species to their environment.
D) His *On the Origin of Species* described man's evolution from animal origins through natural selection.
E) His *On the Origin of Species* was censored and banned by the British government in 1859).

The correct answer is C:) He documented how natural selection governed the adaptation of species to their environment. Charles Darwin's *On the Origin of Species by Means of Natural Selection* exhaustively cataloged numerous plants and animals that had evolved over a long period of time from earlier and simpler forms of life.

103) Which of the following was NOT a result of Stalin's Five Year Plans?

A) Improvement of transportation networks
B) Tripled production of oil, coal and steel
C) Food rations lasting for thirty years
D) Improved military ability and weapon production
E) All of the above are results of the Five Year Plans

The correct answer is C:) Food rations lasting for thirty years. Although food rations did exist throughout the first five year plan, they were removed during the second.

104) The dominant literary and artistic movement in the 1850s and 1860s was

A) Romanticism
B) Realism
C) Positivism
D) Modernism
E) Expressionism

The correct answer is B:) Realism. The dominant artistic and literary movement of the 1850s and 1860s was Realism.

105) Which of the following individuals was NOT a part of the Enlightenment?

A) Rousseau
B) Sir Francis Bacon
C) Cesare Beccaria
D) John Locke
E) Machiavellli

The correct answer is E:) Machiavelli. Machiavelli lived during the Renaissance.

106) By the early twentieth century, Germany began to replace Britain as Europe's industrial leader largely because of

   A) Britain's careless and radical changes made to its industries
   B) Germany's pragmatic laissez-faire approach towards industry
   C) Britain's reliance on cartels to invest large sums of money in new industries
   D) Germany's fast growing chemical, heavy electrical equipment, and steel industries
   E) The exhaustion of iron and coal resources in the British isles

The correct answer is D:) Germany's fast growing chemical, heavy electrical equipment, and steel industries. By the early twentieth century, Germany had begun to replace Britain as Europe's leading industrial power on the strength of new manufactures such as chemical and heavy electrical machinery.

107) Which treaty ended the Franco-Prussian War?

   A) Treaty of Frankfurt
   B) Peace of Westphalia
   C) Treaty of Versailles
   D) Paris Peace Treaty
   E) None of the above

The correct answer is A:) Treaty of Frankfurt. The Treaty of Frankfurt was the treaty that ended the Franco-Prussian War on May 10, 1871.

108) Some of the most powerful labor unions of the nineteenth-century were found in

   A) Italy
   B) Germany
   C) France
   D) Italy
   E) Russia

The correct answer is B:) Germany. Germany processed some of the most powerful labor unions of the nineteenth century.

109) By 1900, most primary-level European educational systems were

   A) Free and compulsory
   B) Expensive to operate and charged high tuition
   C) Backward and lacked good teachers
   D) Still based on a medieval era curriculum
   E) Designed to teach trade skills rather than reading and writing

The correct answer is A:) Free and compulsory. By the beginning of the twentieth century, most primary-level educational systems throughout Europe were free and compulsory.

110) Louis Napoleon's Second Empire was brought to an end by

   A) France's defeat in the Franco-Prussian War
   B) The emperor's financial policies
   C) His poor choice of administrators
   D) His defeat by the Austrians
   E) His failure to produce an heir to the imperial throne

The correct answer is A:) France's defeat in the Franco-Prussian War. France's defeat by Germany in the Franco-Prussian War of 1870–1871 ended Louis Napoleon's Second Empire.

111) A key reason for Germany supplanting England as the industrial leader of Europe was

   A) British unwillingness to support and encourage formal technical and scientific education
   B) British decentralization of factory production
   C) German use of gas-powered internal combustion engines to drive all factory production
   D) Massive German importation of skilled British workers
   E) Geography, for German was located on the continent of Europe and England was an island

The correct answer is A:) British unwillingness to support and encourage formal technical and scientific education. One of the key reasons that the Germans supplanted the British as the industrial leader of Europe was that the British, unlike the Germans, were unwilling to encourage formal scientific and technical education.

112) Which of the following statements BEST applies to the Dual Monarchy of Austria-Hungary before World War I?

A) Both Austria and Hungary had working democratic parliamentary systems.
B) The Magyars dominated politics in Austria under Emperor William II.
C) The nationality problem was unresolved and led to strong German and other nationalist movements.
D) Prime minister Count Edward von Taafe was ousted in 1893 by the disgruntled Slavic minorities.
E) The Austrians and the Hungarians granted independence to the Czechs and Serbs.

The correct answer is C:) The nationality problem was unresolved and led to strong German and other nationalist movements. On the eve of World War I, the Dual Monarchy of Austria-Hungary still faced the unresolved nationality demons that had long disturbed the empire.

113) The quantum theory of energy developed by Max Planck raised fundamental questions about

A) The structure of stars and their positions
B) The accepted medieval theories of chemical reaction
C) The relationship between time and space
D) The safe transmission of electrical energy to power modern economies
E) The subatomic realm of the atom and the basic building blocks of the material world

The correct answer is E:) The subatomic realm of the atom and the basic building blocks of the material world. Max Planck's quantum theory of energy raised fundamental questions about the subatomic structure of the atom.

114) Social Darwinism

A) Applied Darwin's theories to the study of society as large
B) Was an effort to explain the problems of society by psychological means
C) Was a scientific sociological explanation of Darwin's biological ideas
D) Was advocated most strongly by Friedrich Nietzsche
E) Was opposed to concepts of racial superiority

The correct answer is A:) Applied Darwin's theories to the study of society as large. Social Darwinism, which developed in the late nineteenth century, represented an attempt to apply Darwin's theories of organic evolution to the study of society at large.

115) The leader of the women's suffrage movement in England was

    A) Louise Michel
    B) Babette Josephs
    C) Emmeline Pankhurst
    D) Octavia Hill
    E) Nancy Astor

The correct answer is C:) Emmeline Pankhurst. Prior to World War, I Emmeline Pankhurst led a radical women's suffrage movement in England.

116) Which of the following best describes the goals of the delegates at the Congress of Vienna?

    A) To maintain the status quo of Europe and avoid future conflict.
    B) To punish Germany severely for its role in World War I.
    C) To distribute the lands in Africa for each delegate's individual benefit.
    D) To redefined the boundaries of the Americas after the Revolutionary War.
    E) None of the above

The correct answer is A:) To maintain the status quo of Europe and avoid future conflict. The main goal of the Congress was one of moderation. In an effort to avoid future disputes and wars they wished to neither reward any country too greatly, or punish too harshly.

117) Theodor Herzl, the leader of the Zionist movement,

    A) Hoped that the creation of a Jewish state in Palestine would protect European Jews from anti-Semitism
    B) Advocated the development of separate Jewish communities in European cities
    C) Argued for European Jews to assimilate by embracing Christianity
    D) Maintained that living conditions for Jews were better in Eastern Europe than in Western Europe
    E) Attempted to increase the numbers of Jewish Europeans through greater evangelical efforts

The correct answer is A:) Hoped that the creation of a Jewish state in Palestine would protect European Jews from anti-Semitism. In 1896, Theodor Herzl published A Jewish State in which he stated that "the Jews who wish it will have their state" in Palestine. However, Palestine was a part of the Ottoman Empire at that time, and the Ottomans were opposed to Jewish immigration to Palestine.

118) The Boer War was fought by the British in

   A) Nigeria
   B) Northern Rhodesia
   C) Kenya
   D) Botswana
   E) South Africa

The correct answer is E:) South Africa. The Boer War was fought in South Africa between the British and the Boers, Afrikaner descendents of seventeenth-century Dutch settlers.

119) The Triple Alliance included which of the following countries?

   A) England, Germany, and Italy
   B) Russia, England, and France
   C) Italy, Turkey, and England
   D) Germany, Italy, and Austria-Hungary
   E) America, Britain, and France

The correct answer is D:) Germany, Italy, and Austria-Hungary. After the Franco-Prussian War lead to the unification of Germany, Bismarck feared France would seek revenge and the return of the provinces of Alsace and Lorraine. Bismarck created a series of alliances to forestall French retribution. The Triple Alliance included Germany, Italy, and Austria-Hungary, although when World War I began in 1914, Italy chose not to join Germany and Austria-Hungary.

120) Which of the following rulers was considered an enlightened despot?

   A) King Henry VIII
   B) Catherine the Great
   C) Louis XIV
   D) Frederick II
   E) None of the above

The correct answer is B:) Catherine the Great. The three most celebrated enlightened despots were Catherine the Great of Russia, Joseph II of Austria and Frederick the Great of Prussia.

121) In the early twentieth century, the primary antagonists in the Balkans were the

    A) Serbs and Austrians
    B) Russians and French
    C) English and Germans
    D) Serbs and Croats
    E) Ottomans and Germans

The correct answer is A:) Serbs and Austrians. In the early twentieth century, Serbs and the Austrians struggled for dominance in the Balkans.

122) Which scientist the inventor and first to use a telescope?

    A) Ptolemy
    B) Galileo
    C) Copernicus
    D) Kepler
    E) Newton

The correct answer is B:) Galileo. In addition to his studies of planets, Galileo also worked extensive in the field of kinematics.

123) Before the outbreak of World War I, most Europeans were

    A) Highly optimistic and felt material progress would lead to an "earthly paradise"
    B) Indifferent towards the future and lived in the present moment
    C) Extremely negative, and many people believed that the end of the world was near
    D) Happy to let their views be determined by state agencies
    E) Focused on their own families and had little or no knowledge about the outside world

The correct answer is A:) Highly optimistic and felt material progress would lead to an "earthly paradise." In the late nineteenth and early twentieth century, the future seemed bright to most Europeans.

124) The outbreak of the Great War was GREATLY accelerated by the Schlieffen Plan, which

A) Promised full-fledged German support for Austrian military actions against Serbia.
B) Detailed the Black Hand's plan for the assassination of Archduke Ferdinand of Austria.
C) Called for a rapid German invasion France through neutral Belgium before an attack on Russia.
D) Outlined complete Russian mobilization against Germany and Austria-Hungary.
E) Justified Germany's decision to focus most of its military resources in the east against Russia.

The correct answer is C:) Called for a rapid German invasion France through neutral Belgium before an attack on Russia. The Schlieffen Plan called for a rapid German invasion of France through neutral Belgium before turning to fight Russia.

125) The Austrian ultimatum to Serbia precipitated World War I in part because

A) Austria had received unconditional German support for military action
B) England refused to guarantee Serbian territorial integrity
C) France refused to cancel their alliance with the Habsburgs
D) Italy renewed its military alliance with Austria
E) Russia refused to give moral or diplomatic support to the Serbs

The correct answer is A:) Austria had received unconditional German support for military action. The Austrian Government seized upon the assassination of Archduke Francis Ferdinand in Sarajevo to thwart Serbia's Balkan ambitions.

126) Most Europeans believed that the Great War would

A) Be the same length as the American Civil War
B) Be an exciting and patriotic event that would be over in a few months
C) Last years but would not fundamentally realign the map of Europe
D) Result in the unification of Europe as one centralized and highly militarized government
E) Bring a violent Marxist revolution to Europe

The correct answer is B:) Be an exciting and patriotic event that would be over in a few months. Most Europeans believed that the Great War would be over in a few weeks, or months, and supported their government's decision to go to war. Many also believed that the world's complicated industrial economy necessitated a brief war.

127) The usual tactic of trench warfare was to

    A) Surround the enemy and starve him into submission
    B) Use heavy artillery bombardments and then launch direct frontal infantry assaults on well-defended enemy positions
    C) Attempt to outflank the enemy through rapid and mobile deployment of troops and cavalry
    D) Meet the opposing force on the "field of honor" between the trenches for hand-to-hand combat
    E) Avoid any actual combat with the aim of starving the enemy into surrendering

The correct answer is B:) Use heavy artillery bombardments and then launch direct frontal infantry assaults on well-defended enemy positions. The development of trench warfare was unexpected by the generals, and the only plan that they could devise was to launch a long artillery bombardment to flatten the opponent's barbed wire and leave the enemy in a state of disorientation and confusion.

128) After the fall of Napoleon the boundaries of Europe were redefined at the

    A) First European Conference
    B) Paris Peace Conference
    C) Congress of Vienna
    D) Congress of Versailles
    E) Peace of Brest-Litovsk

The correct answer is C:) Congress of Vienna. With the fall of Napoleon it became necessary to remake Europe and restore it to its status before his numerous conquests. This was done at the Congress of Vienna in 1814.

129) The entry of the United States into World War I in April 1917

    A) Gave the nearly-defeated allies a psychological boost
    B) Was greatly feared by the German naval staff
    C) Was a response to Turkey's entrance into the war on the side of the Central Powers
    D) Put an end to Germany's use of unlimited submarine warfare
    E) Was too late to have any impact upon the events of the war

The correct answer is A:) Gave the nearly-defeated allies a psychological boost. On April 1917, the United States joined Britain and France in World War I, in reaction to the unrestricted German submarine warfare.

130) In World War I, the Ottoman Empire fought on the side of

A) Austria and Germany
B) Russia
C) Italy
D) France and Britain
E) America

The correct answer is A:) Austria and Germany. When World War I began in August 1914, the Triple Alliance consisted of Germany, Austria-Hungary, and Italy.

131) Women workers during World War I succeeded by

A) Winning the right to vote immediately following the war
B) Gaining wage equality with men by the end of the war
C) Achieving permanent job security in the once male-dominated workplace
D) Participating in all industries except for textiles
E) Wrestling corporate control of firms from warring men

The correct answer is A:) Winning the right to vote immediately following the war. By necessity, women played a major economic role in World War I, replacing male workers who were in the military.

132) The Russian army's woes during World War I included all of the following EX-CEPT

A) Not enough manpower
B) Poor military leadership
C) Lack of modern armaments
D) Great losses of men in battle
E) Disastrous political leadership

The correct answer is A:) Not enough manpower. When World War I began, Russia was not prepared. Although it had the largest population in Europe and could provide enough soldiers for its armies, Russia lacked modern armaments, military leaders, and was governed by the inept Tsar Nicholas II. By early 1917, the Russian army had suffered three million dead and eight million total casualties.

133) After the Bolshevik seized power in November 1917, Lenin

    A) Accelerated the war effort against Germany
    B) Returned the control of factories to their rightful owners
    C) Ratified the redistribution of land to starving peasants
    D) Successfully managed to reestablish the Duma under socialist control
    E) Inaugurated a worldwide Marxist revolution

The correct answer is C:) Ratified the redistribution of land to starving peasants. After the Bolsheviks seized power in November 1917, Lenin nationalized all land and gave it to rural soviets.

134) All of the following states were created out of the Austro-Hungarian Empire following World War I EXCEPT

    A) Austria
    B) Hungary
    C) Poland
    D) Czechoslovakia
    E) All of the above

The correct answer is C:) Poland. When the Austro-Hungarian Empire disintegrated after World War I, several new states emerged from its wreckage, including Austria, Hungary, and Czechoslovakia. Poland had disappeared from the maps of Europe in the eighteenth century but was reconstituted after the war from mostly Russian but also German territory.

135) The Treaty of Versailles

    A) Fully absolved the Central Powers of guilt for causing the war
    B) Created Wilson's United Nations
    C) Forced Germany to acknowledge "war guilt" and pay reparations
    D) Created a system to dismantle the Turkish Empire
    E) Brought a lasting peace to Europe

The correct answer is C:) Forced Germany to acknowledge "war guilt" and pay reparations. The Treaty of Versailles included Article 231, the so-called War Guilt Clause, which required that Germany accept responsibility for starting World War I.

136) Which of the following was a MAJOR cause of the Great Depression?

   A) European governments were too involved in their own economies.
   B) America recalled its loans from European markets.
   C) Underproduction led to high prices for agricultural goods in eastern and central Europe.
   D) The League of Nations couldn't produce effective economic policies for different economic regions.
   E) German economic difficulties reduced the size of European markets.

The correct answer is B:) America recalled its loans from European markets. Much of Europe's prosperity between 1924 and 1929 rested on massive loans made to Germany by American banks under the Dawes Plan.

137) Mussolini's Fascist dictatorship

   A) Lacked a secret police force
   B) Sponsored highly popular and well attended Fascist youth organizations
   C) Was primarily aimed at aiding the workers and peasants
   D) Never created the degree of totalitarian control found in Russia and Germany in the 1930s
   E) Advanced women's rights and encouraged them to take industrial jobs

The correct answer is D:) Never created the degree of totalitarian control found in Russia and Germany in the 1930s. Although Mussolini's repressive fascist dictatorship used propaganda and created numerous fascist organizations, it never achieved the degree of totalitarian control found in Soviet Russia or Nazi Germany.

138) Which of the following actions would NOT have been characteristic of an enlightened despot?

   A) Naming themselves as a "servant of the state"
   B) Instituting religious tolerance
   C) Promoting education
   D) Centralizing and strengthening their power
   E) Both A and D

The correct answer is D:) Centralizing and strengthening their power. Enlightened despots were heavily influenced by the philosophies of humanism. The term refers to an attitude which these rulers had in which they were more concerned with improving the lives of their citizens than they were in maintaining or exercising power.

139) In *Mein Kampf*, Adolf Hitler

   A) Outlined his plan to take power through a massive rebellion and violent revolution
   B) Told his life story and detailed his ideology of racism, Aryan supremacy, and anti-Semitism
   C) Avoided discussing his anti-Semitism for political reasons
   D) Showed German politicians that he was a dangerous extremist
   E) Was unable to reach German readers because of a ban imposed on the book

The correct answer is B:) Told his life story and detailed his ideology of racism, Aryan supremacy, and anti-Semitism. Hitler wrote his autobiography *Mein Kampf*, or *My Struggle* while in prison for the failed Beer Hall Putsch of November 1923.

140) The only Eastern European nation to maintain political democracy throughout the 1930's was

   A) Bulgaria
   B) Czechoslovakia
   C) Poland
   D) Hungary
   E) Yugoslavia

The correct answer is B:) Czechoslovakia. By the beginning of the 1930s, the only remaining Eastern Europe parliamentary democracy was Czechoslovakia.

141) The collectivization of agriculture under Stalin was characterized by the

   A) Spread of famine caused by peasant hoarding and the slaughter of livestock
   B) Cooperation of kulaks with peasant soviets
   C) Gradual establishment of larger and more efficient collective farms
   D) Rapid improvement of the financial well-being of peasant farmers
   E) Establishment of a widely praised system of large farms granting autonomy to peasant farmers

The correct answer is A:) Spread of famine caused by peasant hoarding and the slaughter of livestock. Stalin's collectivization policy eliminated private farms and moved farming families onto large collective farms.

142) The MOST famous of the surrealistic painters was

   A) Arnold Schonberg
   B) Salvador Dali
   C) Walter Gropius
   D) Wassily Kandinsky
   E) Pablo Picasso

The correct answer is B:) Salvador Dali. Surrealism was an important artistic movement of the interwar years.

143) Which of the following was invented by Eli Whitney?

   A) Steam Engine
   B) Power Loom
   C) Cotton Gin
   D) Battery
   E) Spinning Jenny

The correct answer is C:) Cotton Gin. The cotton gin separated cotton seeds from fibers quickly so that it didn't have to be done by hand.

144) The physicist Walter Heisenberg was MOST noted for

   A) Proposing that uncertainty was at the bottom of all physical laws
   B) Being part of the first team to split the atom
   C) Resurrecting the scientific predictability of classical physics
   D) The development of the atomic bomb
   E) His quantum theory

The correct answer is A:) Proposing that uncertainty was at the bottom of all physical laws. The revolution of physic begun by Einstein and Planck continued into the interwar years.

145) Which of the following was NOT invented before 1800?

   A) Cotton Gin
   B) Steam Engine
   C) Spinning Jenny
   D) Incandescent Light Bulb
   E) Bifocal Glasses

The correct answer is D:) Incandescent Light Bulb. This was invented by Thomas Edison in 1879.

146) The Munich Conference

    A) Was applauded by Winston Churchill as a "wise and noble agreement"
    B) Established that German desires for the Sudetenland necessitated war with
       the Western powers
    C) Was criticized by Winston Churchill as a tragic outcome of appeasement
    D) Represented a severe setback for Hitler
    E) Saved Czechoslovakia from destruction and Europe from another long and
       painful war

The correct answer is C:) Was criticized by Winston Churchill as a tragic outcome of
appeasement. In 1938, Hitler threatened war unless Czechoslovakia ceded the largely
ethnic German territory of the Sudetenland to Germany.

147) Immediately after the fall of Poland,

    A) France and Britain declared war and began an offensive against Germany
    B) France and Britain continued to appease Hitler
    C) The Soviet Union declared war on Nazi Germany
    D) Germany turned on its Russian allies
    E) France and Britain declared war, but remained relatively inactive militarily

The correct answer is E:) France and Britain declared war, but remained relatively inac-
tive militarily. On September 1, 1939, Nazi Germany invaded Poland, using Blitzkrieg,
or "lightning war" tactics.

148) Which ruler said the phrase "L'étât, c'est moi" (I am the state)?

    A) Adolph Hitler
    B) Louis XIII
    C) Louis XIV
    D) James I
    E) Charles I

The correct answer is C:) Louis XIV. Louis XIV, the sun king, used the phrase to show
his absolute rule.

149) The best word to describe absolute rule:

A) Autocracy
B) Democracy
C) Monarchy
D) Republic
E) None of the above

The correct answer is A:) Autocracy. Autocracy means to rule absolutely by either a dictator or a monarch.

Test-Taking Strategies

Here are some test-taking strategies that are specific to this test and to other CLEP tests in general:

- Keep your eyes on the time. Pay attention to how much time you have left.

- Read the entire question and read all the answers. Many questions are not as hard to answer as they may seem. Sometimes, a difficult sounding question really only is asking you how to read an accompanying chart. Chart and graph questions are on most CLEP tests and should be an easy free point.

- If you don't know the answer immediately, the new computer-based testing lets you mark questions and come back to them later if you have time.

- Read the wording carefully. Some words can give you hints to the right answer. There are no exceptions to an answer when there are words in the question such as always, all or none. If one of the answer choices includes most or some of the right answers, but not all, then that is not the correct answer. Here is an example:

The primary colors include all of the following:
A)   Red, Yellow, Blue, Green
B)   Red, Green, Yellow
C)   Red, Orange, Yellow
D)   Red, Yellow, Blue
E)   None of the above

Although item A includes all the right answers, it also includes an incorrect answer, making it incorrect. If you didn't read it carefully, were in a hurry, or didn't know the material well, you might fall for this.

- Make a guess on a question that you do not know the answer to. There is no penalty for an incorrect answer. Eliminate the answer choices that you know are incorrect. For example, this will let your guess be a 1 in 3 chance instead.

Test Preparation

How much you need to study depends on your knowledge of a subject area. If you are interested in literature, took it in school, or enjoy reading then your studying and preparation for the literature or humanities test will not need to be as intensive as someone who is new to literature.

This book is much different than the regular CLEP study guides. This book actually teaches you the information that you need to know to pass the test. If you are particularly interested in an area, or feel like you want more information, do a quick search online. There is a lot you'll need to memorize. Almost everything in this book will be on the test. It is important to understand all major theories and concepts listed in the table of contents. It is also very important to know any bolded words.

Don't worry if you do not understand or know a lot about the area. If you study hard, you can complete and pass the test.

To prepare for the test, make a series of goals. Allot a certain amount of time to review the information you have already studied and to learn additional material. Take notes as you study-it will help you learn the material.

Legal Note

FLASHCARDS

This section contains flashcards for you to use to further your understanding of the material and test yourself on important concepts, names or dates. You can cut these out to study from or keep them in the study guide, flipping the page over to check yourself.

United Provinces	Divine Right/Divine Rule
Huguenots Stuart Dynasty	Stuart Dynasty
Oliver Cromwell took the title of what?	"Principia Mathematica"
The Scientific Revolution's greatest contribution to man was	Tabula rasa

Answer only to God.
Chosen by God to
command the people.

Dutch Republic

James I and Charles I

French Protestants

Newton

Lord Protector

Blank slate

The idea that man is on
a never ending quest to
become perfect

Tabula Rasa was coined by who?	"Spirit of the Laws"
"Letters Concerning the English"	"The Social Contract"
Diderot	"The Wealth of Nations"
Thomas Paine	Despot

Montesquieu

John Locke

Rousseau

Voltaire

Adam Smith

"Encyclopedia"

A rule exercising absolute power

"Common Sense"

Coup d'etat

Napoleonic Code

Decisions reached at
the Congress of Vienna
were based on what three
principles?

Where did the Industrial
Revolution begin?

"Rotten boroughs"

Peace of Paris

Serfdom

Karl Marx

All people are equal under
the law

A sudden takeover of the
government

Great Britain

Legitimacy, the balance of
power, and compensation

Ended the Crimean War

Areas that no longer had
many people but had
kept the same amount
of representation in
Parliament

Founded Socialism

Peasants tied to their land,
in effect slaves for the
landowners

Emmeline Pankhurst	Theodor Herzl
The Boer War	Schlieffen Plan
April 1917	Article 231
Mein Kampf	Salvador Dali

"the Jews who wish it will have their state"

Led a radical women's suffrage movement in England

Rapid German invasion of France through neutral Belgium before turning to fight Russia

Fought in South Africa between the British and the Boers

Part of the Treaty of Versailles, it required that Germany accept responsibility for starting WWI

United States joined Britain and France in World War I

Surrealism

Adolf Hitler

Blitzkrieg	**June 6, 1944**
May 8, 1945	**September 2, 1945**
Holocaust	**Gestapo**
Benito Mussolini	**The Duma**

D-Day

"lightning war" tactics

V-J Day

V-E Day

German secret police

Intentional persecution and systematic murder of European Jews by the Germans

Russia State Legislature

Fascist Party

Treaty of Nanking	"On the Origin of Species by Means of Natural Selection"
Baron Georges Haussmann	Ausgleich
Kaiser	Robert Owen
Charles Fourier	Three items in the triangle trade

Charles Darwin

Granted Britain extensive trading and commercial rights in China

Compromise

Redesigned the city of Paris

Wealthy British manufacturer

Emperor

Slaves, rum & sugar

French philosopher